WORLD
HISTORY SERIES ■ ■ ■

Greek and Roman Theater

Titles in the World History Series

SERIES ■ ■ ■

Greek and Roman Theater

by
Don Nardo

Lucent Books, P.O. Box 289011, San Diego, CA 92198-9011

Library of Congress Cataloging-in-Publication Data

Nardo, Don, 1947-
    Greek and Roman theater / by Don Nardo.
        p. cm.—(World history series)
    Includes bibliographical references and index.
    ISBN 1-56006-249-5 (alk. pap.)
    1. Theater—Greece—History—Juvenile literature. 2. Greek
drama—History and criticism—Juvenile literature. 3. Theater—
Rome—History—Juvenile literature. 4. Latin drama—History
and criticism—Juvenile literature. [1. Theater—Greece—
History. 2. Theater—Rome—History.] I.Title. II. Series.
PA3201.N25   1995
792'.0938—dc20   94-6459
                                                          CIP
                                                           AC

Contents

Foreword

Each year on the first day of school, nearly every history teacher faces the task of explaining why his or her students should study history. One logical answer to this question is that exploring what happened in our past explains how the things we often take for granted—our customs, ideas, and institutions—came to be. As statesman and historian Winston Churchill put it, "Every nation or group of nations has its own tale to tell. Knowledge of the trials and struggles is necessary to all who would comprehend the problems, perils, challenges, and opportunities which confront us today." Thus, a study of history puts modern ideas and institutions in perspective. For example, though the founders of the United States were talented and creative thinkers, they clearly did not invent the concept of democracy. Instead, they adapted some democratic ideas that had originated in ancient Greece and with which the Romans, the British, and others had experimented. An exploration of these cultures, then, reveals their very real connection to us through institutions that continue to shape our daily lives.

Another reason often given for studying history is the idea that lessons exist in the past from which contemporary societies can benefit and learn. This idea, although controversial, has always been an intriguing one for historians. Those that agree that society can benefit from the past often quote philosopher George Santayana's famous statement, "Those who cannot remember the past are condemned to repeat it." Historians who ascribe to Santayana's philosophy believe that, for

example, studying the events that led up to the major world wars or other significant historical events would allow society to chart a different and more favorable course in the future.

Just as difficult as convincing students to realize the importance of studying history is the search for useful and interesting supplementary materials that present historical events in a context that can be easily understood. The volumes in Lucent Books' World History Series attempt to present a broad, balanced, and penetrating view of the march of history. Ancient Egypt's important wars and rulers, for example, are presented against the rich and colorful backdrop of Egyptian religious, social, and cultural developments. The series engages the reader by enhancing historical events with these cultural contexts. For example, in *Ancient Greece*, the text covers the role of women in that society. Slavery is discussed in *The Roman Empire*, as well as how slaves earned their freedom. The numerous and varied aspects of everyday life in these and other societies are explored in each volume of the series. Additionally, the series covers the major political, cultural, and philosophical ideas as the torch of civilization is passed from ancient Mesopotamia and Egypt, through Greece, Rome, Medieval Europe, and other world cultures, to the modern day.

The material in the series is formatted in a thorough, precise, and organized manner. Each volume offers the reader a comprehensive and clearly written overview of an important historical event or period. The topic under discussion is placed in a broad, historical context. For example, *The Italian Renaissance* begins with a discussion of the High Middle Ages and the loss of central control that allowed certain Italian cities to develop artistically. The book ends by looking forward to the Reformation and interpreting the societal changes that grew out of the Renaissance. Thus, students are not only involved in an historical era, but also enveloped by the events leading up to that era and the events following it.

One important and unique feature in the World History Series is the primary and secondary source quotations that richly supplement each volume. These quotes are useful in a number of ways. First, they allow students access to sources they would not normally be exposed to because of the difficulty and obscurity of the original source. The quotations range from interesting anecdotes to far-sighted cultural perspectives and are drawn from historical witnesses both past and present. Second, the quotes demonstrate how and where historians themselves derive their information on the past as they strive to reach a consensus on historical events. Lastly, all of the quotes are footnoted, familiarizing students with the citation process and allowing them to verify quotes and/or look up the original source if the quote piques their interest.

Finally, the books in the World History Series provide a detailed launching point for further research. Each book contains a bibliography specifically geared toward student research. A second, annotated bibliography introduces students to all the sources the author consulted when compiling the book. A chronology of important dates gives students an overview, at a glance, of the topic covered. Where applicable, a glossary of terms is included.

In short, the series is designed not only to acquaint readers with the basics of history, but also to make them aware that their lives are a part of an ongoing human saga. Perhaps they will then come to the same realization as famed historian Arnold Toynbee. In his monumental work, *A Study of History,* he wrote about becoming aware of history flowing through him in a mighty current, and of his own life "welling like a wave in the flow of this vast tide."

Important Dates in the History of Greek and Roman Theater

B.C. 2200	1450	581	550-534	525	501	496	490	485	470	450	430	405	350	3

B.C.

ca. 2200-1450
Minoan civilization on Crete uses religious staging areas that are early versions of theaters.

ca. 850
Epic poems the *Iliad* and the *Odyssey* possibly written and/or performed by legendary bard Homer.

ca. 581
Doric mimes first appear.

ca. 566
Athenian leader Solon initiates *rhapsodia* recitation contests.

ca. 550-534
First formal theater is built in Athens.

ca. 534
Athens first holds the City Dionysia festival; Thespis, the first actor, wins dramatic contest.

525
Playwright Aeschylus is born.

ca. 510
Playwright Phrynichus first wins dramatic contest.

501
Comedies are added to City Dionysia.

499
First version of Theater of Dionysus is built on the slope of the Acropolis in Athens.

496
Playwright Sophocles is born.

ca. 495
Aeschylus introduces the addition of second actor.

490
Greeks defeat Persians at Battle of Marathon.

487
Comedies are officially recognized at City Dionysia.

485
Playwright Euripides is born.

ca. 472
Aeschylus writes *The Persians*.

ca. 470
Sophocles introduces third actor.

458
Aeschylus writes the Oresteia trilogy.

ca. 450
Athenian statesman Pericles initiates fund to provide theater tickets for the poor.

ca. 445
Pericles reconstructs Athens's Theater of Dionysus; comic playwright Aristophanes is born.

ca. 430
Sophocles' *Oedipus the King* is first performed.

414
Aristophanes' *Birds* is first presented.

ca. 405
Euripides writes *Iphigenia in Aulis*.

404
Athens is defeated by Sparta in Peloponnesian War.

ca. 350
Architect Polyclitus the Younger designs Theater of Epidauros.

75 265 240   185 55 A.D. 54-68   200   398 533   1484   1664   1945 1962

ca. 350-300
Atellan farces become popular in Roman Italy.

ca. 342
New Comedy playwright Menander is born.

ca. 330
Theater of Priene is built near Ephesus in Asia Minor.

ca. 275-272
Romans first encounter Greek mimes.

265
Romans complete conquest and unification of Italy.

ca. 254
Roman comic playwright Plautus is born.

240
Roman versions of Greek plays are first presented at *Ludi Romani* festival.

238
Romans establish *Ludi Florales* festival featuring mimes.

ca. 185
Comic playwright Terence is born.

161
Terence's play *Phormio* is produced.

55
Rome's first permanent theater, the Theater of Pompey, is built.

11
Roman emperor Augustus builds Theater of Marcellus in Rome.

A.D.

54-68
Emperor Nero performs his own tragic recitations.

ca. 200
Roman Christian writer Tertullian condemns the theater in his work *On the Public Shows*.

378
Christianity becomes Rome's state religion.

398
Christian leaders threaten to excommunicate followers who attend the theater on church holy days.

476
Rome falls to the northern invaders.

533
Last recorded performance in a Roman theater in ancient times.

1484
Plautus's *The Pot of Gold* is performed for Italian nobles.

1585
Sophocles' *Oedipus the King* is staged in Italian theater copying design of ancient theaters.

1664
French playwright Molière writes *Tartuffe*, based on ancient characters and plots.

1945
Famed actor Laurence Olivier plays Oedipus at London's Old Vic Theater.

1962
Stephen Sondheim's *A Funny Thing Happened on the Way to the Forum*, an adaptation of works by Plautus, opens on Broadway.

The Poetry of Human Conflict

The Greeks, a highly creative people, invented the theater in the sixth century B.C. Beginning in the third century B.C., the Romans, a highly practical people, adapted Greek theatrical plays, characters, and stages to their own needs. Ancient

An ancient Greek mask of tragedy. Wearing a range of such masks, a single actor could portray multiple roles in the same play.

Greek and Roman playwrights and producers established nearly all the theatrical practices and traditions that followed, including those of the present day. The concepts of tragedy, comedy, slapstick, and musical numbers, as well as those of acting, directing, costumes, scenery, raised stages, and even acting awards and the theater ticket all originated with the Greeks and Romans.

To these ancients, especially the Greeks, the theater was not simply a form of entertainment. Because playwrights and actors depicted basic human feelings, emotions, and experiences, the same elements expressed in poetry, theater was a kind of poetry. In its most basic form, poetry depicts, or imitates, natural things or events in written or spoken form. By causing the poet's words to be acted out before an audience, theater also imitates nature and life. The ancient Greek scholar and philosopher Aristotle recognized the element of imitation in poetry and its relationship to the drama of his day. In his *Poetics*, an essay exploring the origins and structure of drama, he stated:

> It is clear that the general origin of poetry was due to two causes, each of them part of human nature. Imitation is natural to man from childhood, one

Tragedy Versus Epic

In his essay entitled Poetics *(quoted here from* The Works of Aristotle*), Aristotle discusses various kinds of poetry and how each relates to drama, especially tragedy. Here he compares the epic poems of Homer to the tragic plays of his own day.*

"Epic poetry . . . has been seen to agree with tragedy to this extent, that of being an imitation of serious subjects in a grand kind of verse. It differs from it *here* however, in that it is one kind of verse and in narrative [story] form; and in its [extreme] length—which is due to its action having no fixed limit of time, whereas tragedy endeavors to keep as far as possible within a single circuit of the sun [the action taking place in the span of a day], or something near that. This, as I say, is another point of difference between them, though at first the practice in this respect was just the same in tragedies as in epic poems. They differ also in their constituents [parts and conventions], some being common to both and others peculiar to tragedy—hence a judge of good and bad in tragedy is a judge of that in epic poetry also. All the parts of an epic are included in tragedy; but those of tragedy are not all of them to be found in the epic."

Aristotle (384-322 B.C.), renowned Greek philosopher, educator, and scientist, wrote about the origins of theater and drama in his Poetics.

of his advantages over the lower animals being this, that he is the most imitative creature in the world, and learns at first by imitation. And it is also natural for all to delight in works of imitation.[1]

Aristotle's view that poetry and a love for it are natural to humans seemed to him to explain why the theater was so popular in his native city of Athens, the cultural center of Greece in the fifth and fourth centuries B.C. Indeed, for Athenians and many other Greeks, poetry was not just one alternative form of literature. It was a means of expression that people grew up with and therefore understood intimately. And that made drama, as a particularly expressive form of poetry, very meaningful to them. Theater scholar Eugene O'Neill Jr. explains:

> For the Athenian of the fifth century B.C., poetry was not alone something which would give him insights into life, but it was likewise an integral and meaningful part of his life. . . . He spent long hours hearing poetry and as a result it became part of his nature. The audiences which witnessed the great [Greek] tragedies must have been made up of individuals who were thus steeped in poetry, for on no other theory can we explain how plays, replete with . . . intricate [poetry] could have been so widely popular.[2]

Another factor that drew the Greeks to drama was that drama, as a form of poetry, was unusually well suited to exploring the conflicts inherent in human nature and in life in general. Unlike many other ancient peoples, the Greeks did not accept the view that their lives were or should be completely controlled by the gods or by godlike kings. The Egyptians and many others tended to accept that their lot in life, however miserable, had been ordained by a higher authority and was therefore beyond their personal control. For the Greeks, by contrast, life was driven by human will. They believed that life's conflicts arise from the choices people make, either for the good or for the bad. This emphasis on human beings and their actions, as opposed to the will of superior beings or powerful individuals, became part of the legacy the Greeks imparted to later cultures. Says theater historian Oscar G. Brockett:

> It was the Greeks who enlarged the human role and established the dominant strain in Western thought, in which humanity . . . is assigned a major share in action and control. . . . Thus, in Western thought the world has come to be seen primarily from the human point of view—that is, as a place of conflict, change, and progress—with humanity as the principal agent both for good . . . and evil.[3]

If people in large degree shape their own destinies, then a character's personal flaws often cause the conflicts that lead to his or her downfall. That concept was repeatedly expressed in the poetry of Greek drama. And all later Western drama, including today's, inherited the idea. Thus, the poetry of human conflict lies at the heart of dramatic entertainment, both ancient and modern. Perhaps it is this element that has always made actors imitating nature and life so appealing.

Chapter

1 Obscurity Gives Birth to Brilliance: The Origins of Theater

The theater as people know it today—actors playing roles before an audience of spectators—was born in ancient Greece. Of that much scholars are sure. However, the exact origins of various theatrical conventions, or basic elements and practices, such as comedy, tragedy, and acting, remain shrouded in mystery. The Greeks, Egyptians, and other ancient peoples left very few written descriptions of themselves and their lives before the sixth century B.C. And of the primitive peoples that preceded them, all that we know is what scientists can deduce from studying bones, crude tools, and other decaying artifacts. So it is not surprising that frustrated scholars find the development of drama difficult to trace. "It is exasperating that the origin of something so significant should be so obscure," comments historian Lionel Casson. "No one knows for certain under what circumstances or precisely when the Greeks got the brilliant idea of having men impersonate imaginary characters."[4]

Stories Told Through Dance

Yet while the exact origins of drama may be obscure, it has been possible to make educated guesses about how people first began acting out certain events from their lives. Anthropologists (scientists who study human cultures) believe that early storytelling was one source of drama. According to this view, primitive hunters may have reenacted their hunting exploits for members of the family or tribe gathered around the campfire, as well as for their gods. In this context, the hunter would

This vase, dated 550 B.C., depicts a Greek hunter, his dog, and their kill.

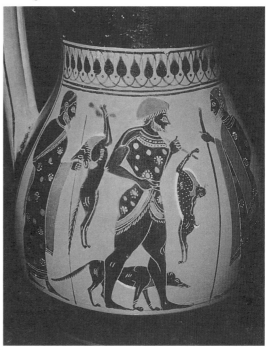

A vase painting showing the god Dionysus, whom the Greeks associated with fertility and recurring cycles such as those of the seasons, birth, and death.

have taken on the role of actor and his listeners that of audience. Such early storytelling probably predated the development of complex language. So, anthropologists believe, initially it likely took the form of dance. As famed theatrical scholar Sheldon Cheney puts it:

> After the activities that secure to primitive peoples the material necessities, food and shelter, the dance comes first. It is the earliest outlet for emotion, and the beginning of the arts. . . . Primitive man, poor in means of expression, with only the rudimentary beginnings of spoken language, universally expressed his deeper feelings through measured movement. . . . He danced for pleasure and as ritual. He spoke in dance to his gods, he prayed in dance and gave thanks in dance. By no means all this activity was dramatic or theatric; but in his designed movement was the germ of drama and of theater. . . . The noises man made, as he rhythmically moved, took on the measure of the swaying body and the tapping feet, gradually became war-

song or prayer, developed into traditional tribal chant, [and] ultimately led to conscious poetry.[5]

In most cultures the poetry of storytelling remained, for the most part, a part of religious ritual. Indeed, in Greece, as in other lands, formal dramatic poetry, along with music and dance, early became associated with religious ceremony. In particular, poetry was prominent in the rituals associated with the god Dionysus. In the early Greek myths, according to Oscar G. Brockett,

> Dionysus was the son of Zeus (the greatest of Greek gods). . . . Reared by satyrs [mythical creatures, half-man and half-goat] he was killed, dismembered, and resurrected. As a god he was associated with fertility, wine, and revelry, while the events of his life linked him with . . . the cycle of the seasons, and the recurring pattern of birth, maturity, death, and rebirth. Through their rites, Dionysian worshippers sought a mystical union with the primal [most primitive] creative

urge. On a more practical level, they sought to promote fertility: to guarantee the return of spring . . . and ample harvests.[6]

The Goat-Song

Worship of Dionysus, along with that of the other Greek gods, developed between the fourteenth and eighth centuries B.C. Little is known about this formative period of the people now referred to as the classical Greeks, whose splendid literature and art of the fifth and fourth centuries B.C. so influenced later civilizations, including today's. What is certain is that by the eighth century B.C. Dionysian ritual had developed a kind of poetry and ceremony known as "dithyramb." This special form of verse, sung and danced to by the worshipers, became the highlight of the religious festivals dedicated to the god. The dithyramb, which told the story of Dionysus or in some way honored him, widened over time to include other gods, as well as some human heroes. The dithyramb also took on an increasingly dramatic form in which a priest led a group of worshipers,

During the yearly festival of Dionysus, worshipers, also known as revelers, take part in the traditional dithyramb procession.

This engraving depicts a family of satyrs, mythical beings, half human and half goat, associated with Dionysus and his revels.

called a chorus, in chanting and dancing before the rest of the congregation. No examples of this verse have survived. But the opening of *The Suppliants*, a play by the fifth-century B.C. playwright Aeschylus [older books often use the spelling Aeschulus], probably captures the general form and atmosphere of the original dithyrambic procession. To the music of flutes and cymbals, a chorus of fifty maidens clad in white robes approaches an altar and rhythmically chants:

Zeus! Lord and guard of suppliant hands!
Look down benign [favorably] on us who crave
Thine aid—whom winds and waters drave [drove]
From where, through drifting shifting sands,
Pours [the river] Nilus to the wave.[7]

Certain men, at first probably priests, became adept at composing new versions

Aeschylus (525?-426 B.C.), the world's first great dramatist, first won Athens's yearly theatrical contest in 484 B.C.

of dithyramb. By creating material specifically to be performed before an audience, they may have been, in a sense, the first playwrights. This is certainly how Aristotle saw it. In his *Poetics*, written in the late fourth century B.C., he theorized that tragedy, the first definite form of drama, originated in Dionysian ritual. Tragedy, said Aristotle,

> certainly began in improvisations [spontaneous pieces] . . . originating with the authors of the dithyramb . . . which still survive . . . in many of our cities. And its advance [as drama] after that was little by little, through their improving on whatever they had before them at each stage.[8]

Supporters of this view point out that the dithyramb was also called "goat-song" be-

cause of the involvement of men dressed as satyrs in the ceremony. The term "tragedy," they say, probably developed from the Greek words *tragos*, meaning goat, and *odi*, meaning song.

The Suspense of Anticipation

Another source of drama in Greece was epic poetry. For centuries, wandering poets known as bards had recited the heroic deeds of gods and human heroes from Greece's dim past. Homer, a legendary bard possibly of the ninth century B.C., was credited with composing the two most famous epic poems, the *Iliad* and the *Odyssey*. The first told the tale of the Greeks' ten-year siege of the powerful kingdom of Troy to rescue Sparta's Queen Helen, who had been abducted by a Trojan prince. The other epic recounted the adventures of the Greek hero Odysseus (or Ulysses) on his way back from the siege.

At first, presentation of the epics was informal. A bard merely stood before a group of townspeople and recited the stories. In time, however, as Greek society became more organized and urbanized, such reciting was more formal. In the eighth and seventh centuries B.C., city-states became the main focus of Greek civilization. Each of these tiny independent nations consisted of a central town and its surrounding villages and farms. By the mid-sixth century, Athens, located on the Attic peninsula in eastern Greece, had become the largest and most influential of the city-states. It had also become the most cultured, with the government spending growing sums to promote the arts and public festivals. In about 566 B.C., seeking to enhance a popular festival, the Athenian leader Solon instituted the *rhapsodia*, contests in which various reciters delivered portions of the *Iliad* and *Odyssey* before a large crowd.

These formal dramatic recitations, like the dithyramb, became very popular with the Athenian populace. Audiences found both presentations exciting and moving, even though they already knew the plots and outcomes. As theater scholar Edmund Fuller explains:

> It is the peculiar power of drama that a play can be utterly gripping to its audience even when everyone knows perfectly well how it is going to end. Indeed, it often draws its greatest force from the fact that we *do* know what is coming. The suspense of anticipation is greater than that of surprise, for the real nature of suspense is anguish, con-

In this eighteenth-century painting, Trojan prince Paris woos Oenone, a nymph, or woodland spirit.

cern for the characters because of our sympathy for them. What fascinates us is how they respond to what happens.[9]

A fanciful depiction of the epic bard Homer, famous for reciting the Iliad *and the* Odyssey.

The First Actor

Later, around 534 B.C., Athens began holding a lavish annual festival known as the City Dionysia, in honor of Dionysus. Both formal dithyramb and *rhapsodia* were presented at this festival, which featured Athens's most popular dramatic contest yet. The first winner of this contest was a poet named Thespis, who developed the dramatic presentations into a new form called tragedy. This first version of what is now recognized as a theatrical play utilized most of the elements of the dithyramb and the *rhapsodia*, but added some important new ideas. Among the innovations of Thespis, for instance, was the addition of a cho-

Song of the Goat

In this excerpt from Stage Antiquities of the Greeks and Romans and Their Influence, *theater scholar James T. Allen explores the origins of the word tragedy.*

"The word tragedy (in Greek—*tragodia*) apparently means goat-song (*tragos*, goat; *odi*, song), but why this name was adopted remains a literary . . . puzzle. Some scholars see in it a reference to the costume worn by the satyrs in . . . dithyrambic performances. Others hold that it arose from the custom of giving in early days [of the dramatic competition] a goat as prize to the victorious poet. Others again ascribe it to the sacrifice of a goat in connection with the ritual. Indeed, more than a dozen different explanations have been proposed. Be the truth in the matter as it may, the name *tragodia* became current [widely used] apparently very early. There came into use also the word *tragodi*, 'goat-singers' or singers of the 'goat-song,' a term employed to signify sometimes 'tragic performance,' sometimes 'tragic troupe,' and, in the singular (*tragodos*) as well as the plural, even 'tragic poet,' 'tragic actor,' and the like. It corresponded roughly to our word tragedian."

rus to the *rhapsodia*. The members of the chorus recited in unison some of the lines and also commented on the events of the story, to focus audience attention more on the passion, plight, and suffering of the heroes. Thespis's other novel idea was actually to impersonate, rather than just tell about, the story's heroes. Theater historian Phyllis Hartnoll states:

The great innovation that Thespis made was to detach himself from the chorus [of both dithyramb and *rhapsodia*] and, in the person of the god or hero whose deeds were celebrated, to engage in dialogue with it. He was thus the first actor as well as the first manager [producer-director]. The step he took was even more revolutionary than it seems to us, for he was the first unsanctified person [non-priest] who dared to assume the character of a god.[10]

In a sense, Thespis created the formal theater overnight. In utilizing dialogue between himself, the first actor, and the chorus, he introduced the basic convention of theatrical plays, namely, characters reciting set speeches, the content of which moves the story along. He also experimented with ways of disguising himself so that he could portray different characters in the same dramatic piece. He eventually decided on masks, which became another basic convention of Greek, and later Roman, theater. In addition, Thespis helped define the role of the audience. By enlarging the dithyramb into a piece of art and entertainment, he transformed the congregation into a true theater audience. For these innovations, Thespis became a theater immortal. As drama historian Marion Geisinger relates:

> The name of Thespis has come down to us in the use of the word *thespian* as a synonym for actor. Actually, the term seems originally to have referred to touring actors, because in ancient Greek vase paintings, Thespis is usually depicted seated on a cart; the tradition was that Thespis would take his actors [chorus members] around in this cart, which they used as a stage or performing platform. Whatever the reason, it seems most fitting to commemorate the first actor in the Western world by dubbing all those who have followed him with his name.[11]

The Early Plays

For subjects, Thespis and the playwrights who adopted his new form of entertainment and competed with him relied on the standard Greek myths, as well as on the tales in the *Iliad* and other epics now lost. They also depicted important recent historical events, especially attacks by the Persians on Greek cities in Asia Minor, what is now Turkey. Unfortunately, none of the plays of Thespis or his contemporaries have survived. Among these writer-actor-managers were Choerilus, who wrote some 160 plays and won the City Dionysia contest thirteen times, and Pratinas, who supposedly wrote 18 tragedies. Phrynichus, another popular writer, first won the contest sometime around 510 B.C. His

Greek musicians and singers chant verses written for a theatrical play.

most famous play was *The Fall of Miletus*, about the Persian takeover of the most prosperous Greek city in Asia Minor. According to the Greek historian Herodotus, this play was so moving that the audience burst into tears and city officials fined Phrynichus 1,000 drachmas, a large sum of money, for upsetting the citizenry.

Although the plays by Phrynichus, Choerilus, and Pratinas are lost, scattered fragments of these works and a few descriptions of them by later writers provide a rough idea of what the performances were like. Scholar James H. Butler, in *The Theater and Drama of Greece and Rome*, fills in some gaps:

> In performance, early Greek tragedies consisted of a series of acted episodes performed by one . . . actor who also conversed with the leader of a chorus. During this action, chorus members reacted in patterned movements and gestures to what was happening. . . . Between episodes the chorus danced, recited in recitative [spoken words with musical accompaniment], and sang choral odes [songs] that related to past events or foreshadowed what was about to happen.[12]

As such performances became increasingly elaborate and dramatic, the City Dionysia festival developed into a major holiday attraction, eagerly awaited each year by the populace. Covering several days at the end of March, the festival was open to all Greeks. The Athenian government wisely took the opportunity to use the celebration as a showcase of Athens's wealth and cultural achievements. To this end, the state financed the theater building and its maintenance, paid fees to the actors, and possibly the

The exaggerated expressions of Greek theatrical masks like this one were plainly visible to the most distant spectators.

playwrights, and also provided prizes for the dramatic contests. All the other expenses of play production were the responsibility of the *choregi*, well-to-do Athenians asked by the state to help with the festival. These citizens were chosen by lot each year, and each *choregus* was assigned to a specific playwright. As Marion Geisinger explains:

> The *choregus* paid for the costumes, the sets, the training of the chorus, whatever supers (non-speaking extra roles) were required by the script, and the musicians. Obviously, the assignment of a generous *choregus* was an advantage to a playwright; that of a niggardly [cheap] one, a disadvantage. . . . Unhappy playwrights often felt that their failure to win the competition at the festival was the result of

The Fleeing Maidens

The opening scene of Aeschylus's The Suppliants *(quoted here from* The Complete Greek Drama*) is a choral procession and song. The chorus is made up of fifty maidens, daughters of Danaus, brother of Aegyptus and son of the god Zeus and the mortal priestess Io. Fearing death at the hands of the sons of Aegyptus, whose marriage proposals they had rejected, the maidens are escaping to the Greek state of Argos, homeland of their grandmother Io.*

Zeus! Lord and guard of suppliant hands!
  Look down benign [favorably] on us who crave
  Thine aid—whom winds and waters drave [drove]
From where, through drifting shifting sands,
  Pours [the river] Nilus to the wave.
From where the green land, god-posset [god-given],
Closes and fronts the Syrian waste [desert],
We flee as exiles yet unbanned
By murder's sentence from our land;
But—since Aegyptus has decreed
His sons should wed his brother's seed,—
Ourselves we tore from bonds abhorred [hated],
From wedlock not of heart but hand [forced marriage],
Nor brooked to call a kinsman lord!
And Danaus, our sire and guide,
The king of counsel [best of advisers], pondering well
The dice of fortune as they fell,
Out of two griefs the kindlier chose,
And bade [advised] us fly [flee], with him beside,
Heedless what winds or waves arose,
And o'er [over] the wide sea waters haste [hurry],
Until to Argos' shore at last
  Our wandering pinnace [ship] came—
Argos, the immemorial home
Of her from which we boast to come—
Io, the ox-horned [headdress] maiden, whom,
After long wandering, woe, and scathe [hard times],
Zeus with a touch, a mystic [magic] breath,
  Made mother of our name.

their being unable to mount their works properly, owing to the assignment of a stingy *choregus*.[13]

The playwrights themselves also had weighty duties. In addition to writing plays, they acted in them, trained the chorus, composed the music, staged the dances, and supervised all other aspects of production. In fact, they were so involved in instructing others that at the time they were known as *didaskali*, or teachers.

Oscar Night in Athens

The playwrights rehearsed their works for months, right up until the beginning of the festival. On the first day, they, their *choregi* and chorus members, along with important public officials, took part in a stately and majestic procession. This colorful parade wound its way through the city and ended at the Theater of Dionysus, at the foot of the Acropolis, the stony hill on which the city's main temples and public buildings rested. After the public sacrifice of a bull to Dionysus, the dramatic competitions began. First came the dithyrambic contests. Then, over the course of the next few days, each of three playwrights presented three tragedies. In the late sixth century B.C., tragedy was still the main dramatic form, as comedy was not yet well developed or popular. When comedies eventually began to be performed at the City Dionysia in 501 B.C., they took place at night, after day-long presentations of tragedy.

The most eagerly awaited moment of the festival was the awards ceremony, in many ways an ancient counterpart of today's Oscar night. Lionel Casson states:

> A panel of ten judges issued four lists containing, respectively, the order in which they rated the tragic playwrights, comic playwrights, tragic leading actors, and comic leading actors. The victors—and that meant those who topped the lists; only first place really counted—were crowned with ivy, and the *choregi* hurried off to arrange farewell banquets for their casts.[14]

As popular and exciting as these early festivals were, they were merely a prelude to what was to come. In the fifth century B.C. Athens produced a brief but magnificent burst of cultural activity, the brilliant results of which would thrill and awe the world ever after. Among the city's artists were a handful of gifted playwrights who would in a stroke create the model for great theater for all times.

Chapter

2 Gods from the Machine: Greek Theatrical Production

As their early theaters and dramatic presentations evolved, the Greeks developed most of the aspects and conventions of play production that became standard through the ages. Among these were the use of scenery, costumes and disguises, chorus, dancing, and music, as well as acting styles and special visual and sound effects. The Greeks also built the first permanent theaters, some of which are still in use. All the theaters in later Western societies, from Rome to the present day, have employed variations of the basic physical layout devised by the Greeks.

We will never know exactly how the Greeks used these theatrical conventions and how their plays appeared on stage. The last authentic Greek productions were presented more than two thousand years ago. And later cultures, beginning with the Romans, modified the original Greek stagecraft to suit their own situations and tastes. Yet modern scholars have carefully studied drawings on Greek vases,

This Greek krater, or mixing vessel, now in an Italian museum, bears a scene of two theatrical characters interacting on stage.

Views of two sections of the ruined Minoan palace at Knossus on Crete: the pillared North Entrance (left), and the theatrical area with its rectangular court and tiers of steps.

many of which depict actors in costume and other theater scenes. They have also sifted through literary descriptions by Greek writers and archaeological evidence from the sites of ancient theaters. Using these clues, scholars have been able to piece together what should be a reasonably accurate picture of how Greek productions were staged.

The World's First Theater

The earliest versions of what eventually developed into theaters for play production were staging areas for religious ceremonies and celebrations. The first known example, and probably the oldest theater in the world, is in the palace at Knossus in northern Crete, the large island located southeast of the Greek mainland. This magnificent building was once the center of the main city in the empire of the Minoans, an early Greek-speaking people who inhabited Crete and many other Greek islands between 2200 and 1450 B.C. By the time of the classical Greeks, Minoan civilization had long since vanished. Yet Minoan persons and events became key elements in classical Greek mythology. And many classical Greek cultural and religious practices had their roots in Minoan times.

The theatrical area at Knossus gives evidence of one such religious practice—the use of formal dancing and singing to honor the gods. In this area, stately and colorful religious rites, very likely similar to the later dithyramb, took place. The area

Ruins of the Theater of Dionysus in Athens, showing the circular orchestra area and part of the seating area, or theatron.

consists of a rectangular court, roughly 40 by 35 feet in size, and paved with large irregular stones. The court is bordered on the east and south by steps on which, scholars believe, the spectators stood and sat. Greek archaeologist Anna Michailidou gives us this description:

> At the south-east corner of the Theater, in the angle between the two banks of steps, there is a bastion-like structure which is believed to have been a sort of royal box for the king and his family. We can imagine the monarch sitting there, surrounded by as many as 500 members of his court standing on the low steps, and watching the . . . dances or religious rites.[15]

The influence of the theatrical area at Knossus and similar areas at other Minoan palaces on later Greek theater design remains unclear. But it is likely that the basic concept of such ritual staging areas survived and became incorporated into the dithyramb in classical times. As the dithyramb evolved into formal theater in the sixth century B.C., the Greeks enlarged and modified these areas to accommodate play production.

Classical Greek Theaters

The first formal Greek theater was built in Athens between 550 and 534 B.C. Its exact location and physical layout are unknown, since the Athenians built over the site when larger theaters came into use a few years later. However, some evidence suggests that the first theater consisted of the same basic elements found in the Minoan versions, although considerably expanded. The rectangular court became the circular orchestra, or "dancing place," where the actors and chorus, as well as members of the dithyrambic processions, performed. And replacing the king's box was a central *thymele*, an altar for sacrificing to and honoring the gods. Surrounding much of the orchestra were wooden bleachers for the audience. The later

Greek scholar Suidas reported that the bleachers collapsed in the middle of a performance, killing several spectators, about the year 499 B.C.

After this unfortunate incident, the Athenians built the Theater of Dionysus against one side of the Acropolis. In its initial form, the theater had an orchestra some 85 feet in diameter with a *thymele* in the center. To avoid another disaster, the seating consisted of wooden planking covering earthen tiers carved into the hillside. In a later renovation, the wooden seats were replaced by the stone versions that have endured to the present. This audience area, which could accommodate more than 14,000 people, became known as the *theatron*, from which the word *theater* comes. On either side of the semicircular *theatron* were the *parodoi*, entrances into the orchestra area used by actors and chorus.

Early in the fifth century B.C. the theater's designers added a structure called the *skene* in front of and facing the orchestra and *theatron*. The word *skene* originally meant "scene building" and is the source of the word "scene" so often used today in stage and film presentations. The original scene building, according to scholar James T. Allen,

> served in the first instance as a background for the actors and provided accommodations for dressing-rooms and perhaps also for the storing of various properties [stage props]. It was of a rectangular shape, sometimes with projecting wings known as *paraskenia* . . . at the sides . . . and it was seldom, if ever, more than two stories in height. Originally constructed of wood or of other perishable materials the scene-building was at first temporary

in character; apparently not until the fourth century was a *skene* of stone erected.[16]

Later, other theaters copying the Dionysus arena's design appeared across Greece. The most beautiful and best preserved is the Theater of Epidauros, located about 110 miles southwest of Athens. Built around 350 B.C. by the architect Polyclitus the Younger, the stone structure is 387 feet across; it has a top seating tier 74 feet above orchestra level and a seating capacity of 14,000. The Epidauros theater remains in such good condition that the Greek National Theater and other modern dramatic companies still perform in it.

The orchestra area of the Theater of Epidauros, the best preserved classical theater in Greece.

The Performers

It was through the *parodoi* in theaters like those of Dionysus and Epidauros that the choruses marched in the opening scenes of the ancient plays. As James Butler explains:

> The usual tragic and comic choruses entered singing the *parodos* (entrance song) and led by a flute player. They were grouped in a rectangular marching formation composed of ranks and files—three by five for tragedy and four by six for comedy. Once in position in the orchestra, they turned and faced the spectators, still singing and gesturing.[17]

During the performance that followed, the chorus members broke formation, moved from place to place, and reacted to the play's events and characters with appropriate verses and gestures. The chorus remained within the orchestra area until the finale, at which time it filed out, once more in formation and singing.

The chorus served several functions. First, it interacted with the actors, giving advice, asking questions, and expressing opinions. In Aeschylus's *The Persians*, for example, the chorus asks Persia's King Xerxes, whose armies the Greeks have defeated, "Is all your glory lost?" The king answers, "See you these poor remains of my torn robes?" "I see, I see," the chorus responds. Also, the chorus's singing and movements, which could be happy and animated or somber and morose, set the overall mood of the play and heightened the dramatic effect. In addition, says Oscar Brockett, the chorus served "an important rhythmical function, creating pauses or retardations [slowing down the action] during which the audience [could] reflect upon what had happened and what was to come."[18]

The actors who interacted with the chorus wore elaborate masks that covered the whole head, resting on the shoulders.

This vase painting shows chorus members from a Greek comedy. The presence of the flute player indicates that both "horses" and riders sang and danced to their lines.

Persia's Glory Lost

CHORUS

O wo, wo, wo! Unspeakable wo
  The demons of revenge have spread . . . .

XERXES

Dismay, and rout, and ruin, ills that wait
On man's afflicted fortune, sink us down.

CHORUS

Dismay, and rout, and ruin on us wait,
And all the vengeful storms of Fate:
  Ill flows on ill, on sorrows sorrows rise;
Misfortune leads her baleful [mournful] train;
  Before the Greek squadrons [fleets] Persia flies,
Or sinks engulfed [drowned] beneath the main [sea].
Fallen, fallen is her imperial power,
And conquest on her banners waits no more.

XERXES

At such a fall, such troops of heroes lost,
How can my soul but sink in deep despair!
Cease your sad strain [comments].

CHORUS

Is all your glory lost?

XERXES

See you these poor remains of my torn robes?

CHORUS

I see, I see. . . . I thought these Greeks shrunk appalled
At arms [were afraid to fight].

XERXES

No: they are bold and daring: these sad eyes
Beheld their violent and deathful deeds.

CHORUS

The ruin, you say, of your shattered fleet?

XERXES

And in the anguish of my soul I tore
My royal robes.

CHORUS

Wo, wo!

The original versions of these reconstructed Greek theatrical masks were worn by comedic actors portraying older men.

Made of linen stiffened with clay and brightly painted, each mask represented a stock character, such as a young maiden, a middle-aged man, an evil king, or a certain god. Writing in the second century A.D., the Greek scholar Julius Pollux listed and described many standard Greek theatrical masks. For example, for tragedy there were six for old men, eight for young men, three for male servants, and eleven for various women; and for comedy, nine for older men, eleven for younger men, seven for male servants, and seventeen for women. Special masks for gods, as well as for satyrs and other mythical creatures, were also used. Comments scholar Bernard M.W. Knox:

> The masks certainly ruled out the play of facial expression which we regard today as one of the actor's most important skills, but in the Theater of Dionysus, where even the front row of spectators was sixty feet away from the

stage (the back rows were three hundred feet away), facial expression could not have been seen anyway. And the masks had a practical value. They made it possible for the same actor to play two or even three or four different parts in different scenes of the play.[19]

The masks also made it possible for men to play women's roles, an important and closely observed convention in ancient Greek theater. Apparently the Greeks considered it improper for women to bare their emotions, even staged ones, in public.

While the masks may have prevented the actors from utilizing facial expressions, they did not limit the use of voices. According to Oscar Brockett:

> The Greeks seem to have placed considerable emphasis upon the voice, for they judged actors above all by beauty of vocal tone and ability to adapt manner of speaking to mood and charac-

ter. . . . The plays demanded three kinds of delivery: speech, recitative, and song. As the primary means of expression, the voice was trained and exercised by the actor much as it might be by an opera singer today. While the best actors attained high standards of vocal excellence, others apparently ranted and roared.[20]

Costumes, Props, and Scenery

Like the masks, Greek theatrical costumes were brightly colored. This was partly to catch the eye from a distance, since most of the spectators sat so far from the actors. Another function of the bright colors was to aid in character recognition. Women's gowns, for instance, were usually of a particular color. A queen's costume was almost always purple, the traditional color of royalty, so that the spectators, who had no programs, could instantly recognize the character. Costume color also denoted mood. A character in mourning or undergoing extreme misfortune, for example, would wear black. In general, says theater historian H.C. Baldry, the actor's "own physical identity was completely concealed: mask, costume and footwear together covered him entirely except for his hands. His robe was usually ankle-length."[21]

The actors also used props, as they do today, although the Greeks tended to use them sparingly. The most common examples were chariots, statues of gods, couches, shields and swords, and biers on which dead bodies were displayed. Special props were also associated with specific characters. Marion Geisinger states:

To differentiate among the gods and the heroes, certain easily recognizable properties were carried. Apollo [the sun god] carried his bow, Hermes [god of invention] his magic wand, Hercules [a heroic strongman] carried his club and lion skin, and Perseus [a clever hero] his cap of darkness. Warriors usually appeared in full armor, with a short scarlet cloak draped around the arm. An old man would carry a staff; a messenger of good tidings wore a crown of olives or of laurel. A king would carry a spear and wear a crown.[22]

While costumes and props tended to be fairly realistic, Greek theatrical producers left the settings largely to the

This 1736 copper engraving shows two Greek actors wearing standard comedic masks and costumes.

In Camei

audience's imagination. This was partly because the design of the open-air theaters placed a strict limitation on the kinds of setting a playwright could depict. In classical times, as a rule, the action of the plays took place outdoors, in front of a house, palace, temple, or other familiar structure. Once added to theaters, the fixed *skene*, redecorated appropriately by the producer, represented the fronts of these buildings. Interiors could not be shown, and there is no solid evidence for the existence in early Greek theaters of painted scenery like that used today.

A modern painting depicts a scene from a Greek theatrical performance.

Special Effects

Partly to overcome the inability to show interiors, in the late fifth century B.C. the Greeks introduced the *eccyclema*, or "tableau machine." Violent acts such as murders were almost always committed "indoors," and therefore offstage and out of sight, and the audience learned about them secondhand from messengers and other characters. Sometimes, however, to achieve shock value, a doorway in the *skene* would open and stagehands would push out the *eccyclema*, a movable platform on rollers. On the platform, frozen in a posed and dramatic tableau, would be usually both murderer and victim. In the climax of productions of Aeschylus's play, *Agamemnon*, for example, an *eccyclema* probably displayed the body of the slain king. Standing over Agamemnon's corpse was his wife and killer, Clytemnestra, weapon in hand. Despite knowing full well this scene was coming, the spectators usually gasped in horror.

The Greeks developed special theatrical effects of other kinds to heighten the stage spectacle. Julius Pollux described a *keraunoskopeion*, or "lightning machine," and a *bronteion*, or "thunder machine," but unfortunately he did not explain how these devices worked. Perhaps the most spectacular engine of special effects was the *machina*, from which the word "machine" is derived. As Eugene O'Neill Jr. explains, "Frequently at the close of a play the dramatist introduced a god into the action, who would naturally be expected to appear from above. He apparently was brought in by some kind of crane or derrick, called the 'machine.'"[23] This mechanical arm probably was raised by ropes

The Goddess Speaks

The playwright Euripides used the deus ex machina, or "god from the machine," in his play Iphigenia in Tauris. *In this excerpt from the climax (quoted in* The Complete Greek Drama), *Athena, goddess of war and wisdom, appears and addresses Thoas, king of Tauris, who is pursuing Orestes and other Greek intruders in his land.*

THOAS

Inhabitants of this barbaric land [Tauris],
Will you not rein your steeds, will you not fly
Along the shore, to seize whatever this ship
Of Greece casts forth; and, for your goddess roused,
Hunt down these impious [bad] men? . . .

(Athena appears above)

ATHENA

Where, O royal Thoas, do you lead
This vengeful chase? Attend [listen]: Athena speaks.
Cease your pursuit, and stop this rushing flood
Of arms; for here, by the fateful voice
Of Phoebus [a sun god], came Orestes, warned to fly
The anger of the Furies [vengeful winged creatures], to
  convey [take]
His sister Iphigenia to her native Argos back,
And to my land [Greece] the sacred image bear.
Thoas, I speak to you . . . [do not be] angry.

THOAS

Royal Athena, he that hears the gods
Commanding, and obeys not, is unwise. . . .
My arms I will restrain, which I had raised
Against the strangers, and my swift-oared ships,
Since, potent [powerful] goddess, this pleases you.

ATHENA

I praise your resolution; for the power
Of fate over you and over the gods prevails.

---

and pulleys, and the actor playing the god dangled from it on a hook.

The *machina* was also used to show spectacular human exploits, such as the hero Bellerophon riding the flying horse Pegasus. Comedy writers and producers used the *machina* in a humorous way. In Aristophanes' play *Peace*, for instance, a nonheroic farmer flew a giant dung beetle over the orchestra and *skene* and shouted, "Hi, crane-operator, take care of me!" Invariably, though, most playwrights used the device to fly in gods for the finale, an approach that eventually became overused. O'Neill comments, "The term *deus ex machina*, 'the god from the machine,' has become standard in dramatic criticism. It . . . refers to awkward, mechanical, and unconvincing means which a playwright is forced to employ if he cannot work out a satisfactory resolution to his plot."[24]

Caught Up in the Excitement

All these theatrical elements—masks, costumes, machines, and the like—were designed to entertain the audience. The playwrights and producers demonstrably attained this goal, for the theater was immensely popular in Greece. In Athens in the fifth century B.C., for example, performances were always sold out. The Athenians, it seems, also invented the theater ticket. This was necessary because nearly all the city's 200,000 or more people desired entrance into a building that seated no more than 17,000 at its largest expansion. Yet playgoing was not exclusively a pastime of the well-to-do. About the year 450 B.C., the democratic leader Pericles instituted a special government fund to provide tickets for the poor.

Greek theater audiences differed from modern ones mainly in their outward show of enthusiasm. As James H. Butler puts it:

If it were possible to project ourselves back in time, to attend a series of performances at one of the great festivals given in the Theater of Dionysus, the strongest impressions we would have,

aside from those caused by strange scenic and acting conventions, would be of the audience. For they were caught up in a feverish excitement, an intense interest in the outcome of the various contests. Their volatility and enthusiasm were more characteristic of present-day football and baseball spectators than of the quiet . . . often passive demeanor exhibited by our theater audiences. The hundreds directly competing for prizes and honors in the City Dionysia sharpened the appetite for victory. Add to this group several hundred, perhaps several thousand, former chorus members, dithyrambic performers, flute players, and extras sprinkled among the audience. They had competed in previous festivals and were quite knowledgeable on the finer points and techniques of performance. Refreshments to sustain the "dawn to dusk" audience were hawked [sold by roving vendors], thereby increasing the general noise and commotion.[25]

Greek audiences differed from today's in another way. Because the Greeks invented the theater, their audiences witnessed something unique, an institution that existed nowhere else and developed and evolved before their eyes. Theatrical conventions and ideas that today seem run-of-the-mill were, in ancient Athens, fresh and exciting. It was in this stimulating, creative atmosphere that some of the greatest playwrights of all time worked their magic.

Chapter

3 Tragedy's Three Giants: The Golden Age of Greek Drama

In the first years of the fifth century B.C., Thespis and his Athenian colleagues, theater's pioneers, gave way to new generations of playwrights and actors. After Athens's theater building moved to the

The right front corner of the famed Parthenon atop Athens's Acropolis.

area known as the Precinct of Dionysus on the slope of the Acropolis in 499, more people than ever attended performances. Many of these theatergoers came from other Greek city-states as the Athenian drama festivals increasingly gained a reputation for splendor and excellence unmatched anywhere else.

Politics and economics played indirect roles in this flowering of dramatic art in Athens. The city had begun the century already the largest and wealthiest state in Greece. Then the Athenians gained a tremendous surge of prestige and power during Greece's heroic and crushing defeat of the Persian Empire. First in 490, and again in 480, huge Persian invasion forces landed in Greece. Leading the Greeks in decisive victories at Marathon and Salamis, Athens established itself as the country's savior and reaffirmed its status as the foremost city-state. In the following decades, the Athenians used their status and influence to build an empire. Cities and islands stretching from Greece to Italy and other Mediterranean lands came under their control, and Athens acquired vast power and wealth.

The Athenians poured a great deal of their new wealth into cultural endeavors. It was during this period, for instance, that they built the magnificent Parthenon and

TRAGEDY'S THREE GIANTS: THE GOLDEN AGE OF GREEK DRAMA ■ **35**

The Eternal Struggle

This miniature Greek tragic mask, constructed of clay, dates from the third century B.C.

Several different theatrical styles, including comedy, flourished in the cultural renaissance between 500 and 400 B.C. Yet tragedy, especially in the hands of the three giants, remained the highest expression of dramatic art. Perhaps this preoccupation with grand and serious themes came from the unique way the Greeks, particularly the Athenians, viewed life. Athens was the birthplace of democracy and human freedom, and its form of government influenced democratic reforms in other Greek city-states. Unlike people in other lands at the time, the Greeks enjoyed not only freedom of action and association, but also freedom of thought. In the words of famed classical scholar Edith Hamilton:

> Tragedy was a Greek creation because in Greece thought was free. Men were thinking more and more deeply about human life, and beginning to perceive more and more clearly that it was bound up with evil and that injustice was of the nature of things. And then one day, this knowledge of something [inherently] wrong in the world came to a poet with his poet's power to see beauty in the truth of human life, and the first tragedy was written.[26]

Thus, the Greeks were the first to recognize clearly one of life's great contradictions. They saw the reality that ugliness and beauty inevitably coexist in the world: that each, by sharp contrast, defines the other. They realized that to find and embrace the good, one must accept, confront, and deal with the bad. According to scholar Paul Roche:

other temples on the summit of the Acropolis. Architecture, sculpture, painting, and literature thrived as the government supported the arts and attracted the brightest and most talented individuals from the Greek world. Amidst this unprecedented cultural outburst, Greek theater continued its rapid evolution. Among the many fine playwrights were three giants—Aeschylus, Sophocles, and Euripides. Through them, drama reached heights of expression, structure, and emotional impact that have never been surpassed, peaks of excellence that have profoundly influenced dramatists through the ages.

Greek actors in their dressing rooms within the skene *select their masks in preparation for a tragic performance.*

The theme of all tragedy is the sadness of life and the universality of evil. The inference the Greeks drew from this was *not* that life was not worth living, but that because it was worth living the obstacles to it were worth overcoming. Tragedy is the story of our existence trying to rear its head above the general shambles [life's darker elements].[27]

And it was this eternal struggle, humanity's attempt to find light in darkness, beauty in ugliness, that the Greek tragedians explored in their plays. "In tragedy," says Edith Hamilton, "the Greek genius penetrated farthest and it is the revelation of what was most profound in them."[28]

Purging the Emotions

The tragic playwrights attempted to achieve three basic goals in their writing. First, they tried to show that humans possess free will and, therefore, are responsi-

ble for their own actions. According to this view, people have the choice of doing good or bad deeds, and exercising that choice reveals a person's character. Typically, making the wrong choice plunges a person into despair and tragic circumstances. Second, the tragedians endeavored to show that a divine or superhuman power or force exists above humanity. It might be a god or gods, or it might be fate or destiny. Although such a higher power does not control people like puppets, it does partially determine their actions, and ultimately they must answer to it. Often, the higher power appeared at the end of a play, as a deus ex machina, forcing the characters to reckon with it.

The tragic writers' third goal was to help the audience members achieve a catharsis—a purge, or release, of pent-up anxiety and emotions, which ultimately calmed and satisfied those who experienced it. In fact, Aristotle stressed the importance of catharsis in his definition for tragedy. "A tragedy," he wrote in his

Poetics, "is the imitation of an action that is serious . . . with incidents arousing pity and fear, with which to accomplish its catharsis of such emotions."[29] Catharsis works as the spectators watch the characters on stage make their tragic mistakes and pay the penalties for their actions. The members of the audience, having made their own mistakes in life, identify with the characters' plight and at the end feel, along with the characters, relief that the strife is over. The extreme seriousness of the situations depicted in the Greek tragedies was, no doubt, an added source of relief. On the way home from watching *Medea*, in which a mother murders her children, an Athenian theatergoer likely felt fortunate that his or her own problems were far less serious.

Aeschylus's Grand Style

Sixth-century B.C. playwrights like Thespis and Phrynichus had achieved catharsis and the other goals of tragedy to a limited degree. It was not until the early fifth century, however, that Aeschylus, the first major theatrical innovator after Thespis, brought the tragic art to the level of great literature. In a sense, Aeschylus created the version of the tragic play as the world now understands tragedy.

Born perhaps about 525 B.C., Aeschylus fought both at Marathon and Salamis and witnessed the rise of Athens to political and cultural greatness. These epic events became major themes of his plays. For example, *The Persians*, written about 472 B.C., and the oldest surviving complete tragedy, depicts with a compelling sense of immediacy the sweeping Greek victory over Persia. Of the ninety plays Aeschylus reportedly wrote, eighty-two titles are known, but only seven complete manuscripts survive. Besides *The Persians*, these are *The Seven Against Thebes*, written in 467; the Oresteia, a trilogy consisting of *Agamemnon*, *The Libation Bearers*, and *The Eumenides* (458); *The Suppliant Maidens* (ca. 463); and *Prometheus Bound* (ca. 460). Aeschylus won his first victory in the City Dionysia dramatic contests in 484 and went on to win twelve more times.

One of Aeschylus's great innovations was the introduction of a second actor. Until his time, playwrights made do with one actor who interacted with the chorus in various ways. But this format limited writers to telling fairly simple stories with a few characters, which the lone actor attempted to portray using different masks. The addition of a second actor significantly expanded the possibilities open to playwrights, since it allowed the depiction of twice as many characters. Also, as James H. Butler points out, the second actor

> helped broaden and deepen the tragic action, for even as a messenger or herald this actor could vitally alter a hero's position with the type of news he conveyed. Furthermore, this addition of the second actor tended to reduce the importance of the chorus.[30]

Aeschylus also used the trilogy, or series of three related plays, as a way to broaden his scope. By allowing a story to unfold in three successive plays, he was able to show in more detail the evolution and impact of a concept such as justice, greed, or fate. For example, the three plays of the Oresteia, the only Greek trilogy that survives in complete form, trace a repeating pattern of revenge and murder in the family of Agamemnon, king of Argos. At the climax of the third play, the violent cycle is broken when the goddess Athena intervenes.

In presenting such epic and serious themes, Aeschylus utilized grand poetry of amazing beauty and power. On the playwright's style, Paul Roche comments:

The stamp of Aeschulus's soul was loyal, heroic, aristocratic, and uncompromising. . . . What he saw he sent

---

The Chain of Vengeance Broken

In this excerpt from A Pageant of the Theater, *scholar Edmund Fuller summarizes the plot of Aeschylus's epic trilogy, the Oresteia.*

"Agamemnon, king of Argos, was commander-in-chief of the Greek armies [attacking] Troy. He was the brother of Menelaus, king of Sparta, whose wife Helen had run off with Paris, one of the sons of Priam, king of Troy. The war was fought to recover her and lay waste the offending city. The sailing of the Greek armies from the harbor of Aulis [in Greece] was delayed by unfavorable winds. Agamemnon sacrificed his daughter, Iphigenia, to propitiate [appease] the gods and get fair winds. The play [*Agamemnon*, first in the trilogy] opens more than ten years later. A long-awaited signal fire reveals that the war is ended by a Greek victory; Agamemnon is returning. For years, Clytemnestra, his wife, has nursed hatred of him for killing their daughter, and she has plotted against him with her lover, Aegistus. When the king arrives she welcomes him before the palace but then, leading him into his bath, casts a net over him and murders him with an axe. . . . In the second play [*The Libation Bearers*], Orestes, son of Agamemnon, in league with his sister Electra, commanded by the god Apollo, slays his mother Clytemnestra and her lover . . . to avenge his father. The third play is *The Eumenides* . . . . Orestes is haunted by the Furies [supernatural pursuers of persons guilty of unpunished crimes] who demand his death. . . . Orestes [goes] to trial in Athens. The judges divide equally for and against him. Then the goddess Athena . . . intervenes and casts the acquitting vote. She appeases the Furies . . . and decrees that chains of crime and vengeance must be broken."

A scene from Aeschylus's The Seven Against Thebes, *written in 467 B.C., in which seven mighty warriors vow to destroy the walls of the city of Thebes or die.*

[words] flooding out of of him, crashing down in thunderous poetry. . . . His style of writing is all of these things: majestic, flaming, close-packed, loaded [with insight]. . . . It is the grand style par excellence. . . . It is a language that can put us in touch with the human on a divine plane and make us see ourselves as we might or ought to be.[31]

A typical example of this powerful poetry appears in *The Eumenides*, the final play in the Oresteia. The Furies, bloodthirsty supernatural beings, who hunt down and punish the wicked, warn that the guilty cannot escape their bloody wrath:

> None may come besides us gathered
>   round the blood-feast—
> For us no garments white
> Gleam on a festive day; for us a darker
>   fate is,
> Another darker rite. . . .
> On him who slays [a murderer] we
>   sweep with chasing cry:
> Though he be triply strong,
> We wear and waste him; blood atones
>   for blood,
> New pain for ancient wrong.[32]

Sophocles—Master of Character Motivation

Aeschylus was in his sixties when the great Athenian statesman Pericles rose to power about the year 461 B.C. Under Pericles, the government spent unprecedented sums on the arts, and theater flourished as never before. In the mid-to-late fifth century, some of the greatest plays ever written were performed in Athens. Many of these were from the pen of Sophocles, who inherited from Aeschylus, thirty years his senior, the unofficial position of greatest dramatist of the day. Bernard Knox writes:

> Sophocles, son of Sophillus, was born at Colonus, just outside Athens, some time around 496 B.C. He came of a well-to-do family and was given the education of a young aristocrat of the period, which included athletics and music. . . . During his ninety years, he played a distinguished part in public affairs, as general on at least one occasion. . . . But he was known to his fellow citizens mainly as the most

Sophocles (496-406 B.C.), whose career spanned the years in which Athenian culture reached its magnificent zenith.

terization. He was the first to use a third actor, which increased the amount of character interaction in his dramas and gave his characters complex but clear-cut motivations for their actions. By focusing on the characters, he further reduced the importance of the chorus, fixing its size at fifteen members. The plots of Sophocles' plays revolve around characters whose flaws lead to mistakes, which draw them and those around them into crises and suffering. During the climax of a play, the main character recognizes his or her mistake and accepts the punishment meted out by society or the gods. The best and most famous example is the plight of Oedipus in *Oedipus the King*, considered by Aristotle and many critics through the ages to be the greatest of all tragedies. Marion Geisinger explains:

> The action of the play describes how Oedipus gradually comes to realize that he has, in ignorance, killed his father [the former king] and married his

A vase painting showing Sophocles' character Oedipus solving the riddle of the Sphinx.

successful dramatist who had ever presented plays in the Theater of Dionysus. He won his first victory at the tragic festival in 468 B.C., defeating the older poet Aeschulus. . . . This was the start of a career which was to bring him the first prize in the contest no less than eighteen times; he was sometimes awarded the second prize . . . but never, we are told, the third.[33]

Sophocles' impact on the theater was extraordinary. His output of plays was large—reportedly 123 in all—but only 7 have survived. Among these are *Ajax*, written in 442 B.C., *Antigone* (ca. 441), and his masterpiece, *Oedipus the King* (ca. 430). Sophocles concentrated most on charac-

Murder at the Crossroads

In this excerpt from Sophocles' Oedipus the King, *quoted in* An Anthology of Greek Drama, *Oedipus questions his wife, Queen Jocasta, about her former husband, the late King Laius, whom Oedipus has always believed he never met. Now, with growing fear, he is starting to suspect that a troublesome old man he killed on a country road long ago might have been Laius.*

"OEDIPUS: O dear Jocasta, as I hear this from you, there comes upon me a wandering of the soul—I could run mad. I thought I heard you say that Laius was killed at a crossroads.

JOCASTA: Yes, that was how the story went and still that word goes around.

OEDIPUS: Where is this place, Jocasta, where he was murdered?

JOCASTA: Phocis is the country and the road splits there, one of two roads from Delphi, another comes from Daulia.

OEDIPUS: How long ago is this?

JOCASTA: The news came to the city just before you became king and all men's eyes looked to you. What is it, Oedipus, that's in your mind?

OEDIPUS: Don't ask me yet—tell me of Laius—how did he look? How old or young was he?

JOCASTA: He was a tall man and his hair was grizzled already—nearly white—and in his form not unlike you.

OEDIPUS: O God, I think I have called curses upon myself in ignorance. . . . I and no other have cursed myself. And I pollute the bed of him I killed by the hands that killed him. Was I not born evil? Am I not utterly unclean?"

mother. The power of this tragedy is unsurpassed in all literature for the stage. The impact becomes overwhelming when Oedipus, refusing to plead his ignorance, accepts full moral responsibility for his acts, and in a fervor of guilt, blinds himself. Here is flawless structure and high moral purpose.[34]

Oedipus the King also illustrates the beauty of Sophocles' verse. In the following lines, the author captures the main character's anguish as, having blinded himself, he faces two kinds of darkness—that of being sightless and that of remembering his crimes:

O, O, where am I going? Where is my voice borne on the wind to and fro? Spirit, how far have you sprung?. . . Darkness! Horror of darkness enfolding, resistless, unspeakable visitor sped by an ill wind in haste! Madness and stabbing pain and memory of evil deeds I have done![35]

Euripides Questions Traditional Values

When *Oedipus the King* was presented in Athens, Euripides, the third giant of Greek tragedy, was already in his fifties and had competed often with Sophocles in the City Dionysia. Born in 485 B.C., Euripides had his first plays produced in 455. Of a total of some eighty-eight, eighteen have survived, including *Alcestis*, written in 438, *Medea* (431), *Heracles* (ca. 422), *The Trojan Women* (415) and *Iphigenia in Aulis* (ca. 405).

Euripides won the dramatic prize only five times and was far less popular in his own day than either Aeschylus or Sophocles had been in theirs. This was primarily because Euripides often questioned accepted and traditional values. For example, he suggested that life is a series of random events and that the world operates more by chance than under the influence of the gods. In this view, human beings are just as concerned as the gods, or even more concerned, with establishing moral values. Euripides did make gods characters his plays, but usually he confined his use to a single deus ex machina at the end, to wrap up the plot as conveniently as possible.

In exploring how humans shape their own values and destinies, Euripides also depicted ordinary people in highly realistic ways. Many Athenians saw this mode of expression as too undignified for the tragic stage, which they believed should show more heroic people and themes. Euripides was far ahead of his time in his emphasis of real people and corresponding de-emphasis of the gods, and later scholars came to see him as the first playwright to deal with human problems in a modern way.

Euripides' focus on people also made the chorus even less important than it had been under Sophocles. According to scholar Rex Warner, in Euripides' plays:

> The real drama is confined to the men and women taking part in it. The chorus [members] perform the role of

Euripides (485-406 B.C.) was the first playwright to depict human problems in a realistic, modern way.

A Lady of Sorrows

In this speech in Medea (quoted here from The Complete Greek Drama), Medea reveals her intention to do away with her children. Euripides supplies his character with lines so natural sounding that they would not be out of place in a modern film script.

"My friends, I am resolved upon the deed; at once will I slay my children and then leave this land, without delaying long enough to hand them over to some more savage hand to butcher. Needs must they die in any case; and since they must, I will slay them—I, the mother that bore them. O heart of mine, steel yourself! Why do I hesitate to do the awful deed that must be done? Come, take the sword, you wretched hand of mine! Take it, and advance to the post from where starts your life of sorrow! Away with cowardice! Give not one thought to your babes, how dear they are or how you are their mother. This one brief day forget your children dear, and after that lament [mourn them]; for though you will slay them, yet they were your darlings still, and I am a lady of sorrows."

This second-century A.D. statue shows Medea slaying her own children.

sympathetic listeners and commentators, or . . . provide the audience with a kind of musical and poetic relief from the difficulties or horrors of the action.[36]

And indeed, Euripides' plays were filled with horrors—realistic images and ideas his audiences often found strange or abnormal. Among other things, he depicted a woman in love with her own stepson and a maiden feeling passion for a bull. Perhaps most repulsive of all was the scene in *Medea* in which the title character kills her children. The scene is typical not only of the author's powerful themes, but also of his highly realistic, almost modern, style of dialogue. Just before committing the crime, Medea addresses the chorus:

My friends, I am resolved upon the deed; at once will I slay my children

The Theater of Dionysus as it may have appeared in the third or second century
B.C. after the construction of elaborate additions to the skene.

and then leave this land, without delaying long enough to hand them over to some more savage hand to butcher. Needs must they die in any case; and since they must, I will slay them.[37]

The theatrical reign of Aeschylus, Sophocles, Euripides, and their contemporaries was short-lived. In 404 B.C. Athens lost the bloody Peloponnesian War to Sparta, another Greek city-state, and the golden age of Athenian culture ended. Theater and the City Dionysia continued in the fourth century, but tragedy's

great era of innovation and creative output was over. Perhaps authors felt that all that could be said in the tragic genre had been said already. Or maybe audiences' tastes had changed.

The precise reasons for the end of tragic dramas' golden age will never be known. What is certain is that with few exceptions, the tragic presentations the Greeks witnessed in the following centuries were revivals of the works of the fifth-century giants. It is a testament to the greatness of these writers that revivals of these works continue to the present.

Chapter

4

Poking Fun at Life's Absurdities: The Old Comedy

During the years that tragedy developed and flourished in Athens and other Greek cities, theater audiences also enjoyed comedies. Most comedies were burlesques, or slapstick farces filled with silly situations and dirty jokes, both visual and verbal. Usually, the object of comic actors was to be as ridiculous as possible, as Aristotle emphasized in his definition of comedy. "As for Comedy," he wrote, "it is . . . an imitation of men worse than the average . . . but only as regards one particular kind, the Ridiculous, which is a species of the Ugly." [38] Aristotle went on to explain that comedy depicts a kind of ugliness that does not inflict pain, but instead excites laughter.

Greek spectators loved the early comic plays but did not equate them with the tragedies, which they viewed as great art. To the Greeks, the comedies were not important theatrical statements, but merely pleasant interludes of comic relief, to offset the grimness of the tragic presentations. Nevertheless, what theater historians call the Old Comedy, roughly covering the period from 501 to 404 B.C., eventually developed into an art form in its own right. And it became the model for the comic theaters that followed, including those of fourth-century B.C. Greece, Rome, medieval Europe, and even the present day.

Jokes and Bawdy Revelers

The exact origins of comedy are uncertain. Even Aristotle was not sure, explaining that "its early stages passed unnoticed. . . . Who it was who supplied it with masks, or prologues, or a plurality of [several] actors and the like, has remained unknown." [39] Yet both Aristotle and later scholars speculated that the comic plays performed in the Theater of Dionysus in the fifth century B.C. developed from a number of specific sources.

One of these sources was religion. Just as tragedy developed out of the serious aspects of early Greek religious rituals, comedy evolved from the bawdy, or humorously indecent, aspects of these rituals. The Dionysian processions, including the dithyramb, featured groups of worshipers, or revelers, marching and singing. Because these early rites were associated with fertility, the phallus, or penis, which was the principal male fertility symbol, was an important element of the processions. Revelers usually carried large phallic symbols on poles as they marched along.

Most of these processions were of a serious nature. However, sometimes onlookers shouted at the marchers, calling out crude jokes and obscenities, usually relat-

A scene from a Greek satyr-play. These bawdy presentations contained many dirty jokes, obscene dances and gestures, and probably flashes of nudity.

ing to the oversized phalluses. Often the revelers responded with joking insults of their own, and the rite would take on a humorous tone. In time, many Dionysian processions purposely used a comic approach, featuring revelers dressed in animal costumes, particularly goats. These were the satyrs, bawdy revelers who proudly displayed their phalluses and joked, danced, and sang as they marched. That such processions were one important source of comedy is supported by that term's root words—*komos*, meaning "revel," and *aeidein*, meaning "to sing."

The satyr processions influenced the satyr-play, a kind of dramatic presentation that developed in the early years of Athens's City Dionysia. Usually, it was a short comic sketch consisting of jokes ridiculing the gods, heroes, or other aspects of mythology; there was also dancing that featured obscene movements and gestures. According to Sheldon Cheney:

> The touch of the ridiculous that always followed the sublime experience of the tragedy productions in Athens is to be found in the satyr-plays. . . . The satyr drama survived as a separate entity through the entire fifth century. The invariable central feature was the chorus of satyrs, hairy fellows with horns, tails, and phalluses, who could be relied upon to [delight] any audience by their antics. For the rest, there seems to have been the strangest mixture of heroics and buffoonery. Sometimes the tragedies would be followed by one of these ludicrous burlesques in which the very same [characters], heroes and kings, would be seen from a comic angle, brought down to the grotesque and often indecent by-play of rough-and-tumble farceurs [slapstick actors].[40]

All the serious tragedians, including Aeschylus, Sophocles, and Euripides, wrote satyr-plays, usually to provide comic relief for their audiences after the ordeal of tragic catharsis. Only one satyr-play has survived—Euripides' *The Cyclops*—based on an episode from Homer's *Odyssey*.

The Doric Mimes

The Old Comedy also had nonreligious sources and influences. The most important were the Doric mimes, which originated in the mid-sixth century B.C. in the city-state of Megara, located about thirty miles southwest of Athens. The term itself comes from the Greek word *mimos*, meaning "imitator," and the mimes were, in a way, crude imitations of people and events. Essentially, they were comic skits, spoken rather than sung (the idea of a mime actor who does not speak is a more modern development). As James H. Butler explains:

> At first they were improvised, but later they were written down. The term [mime] was interchangeably applied to both actors and plays. Figures on

A Greek vase bears images of acrobats and actors performing in a comic Doric mime.

sixth-century . . . vases depict mime actors wearing short, heavily underpadded costumes . . . several are equipped with masks and huge phalluses. . . . Story material and stock characters for Doric mimes came from two general sources: mythology acted out in burlesque fashion, and comic intrigues drawn from daily life. . . . The ancient mimes (players) who gave "imitations of life" were skilled at more than character and situation portrayal. They also effectively imitated animals and birds, a feature present in many of the later Old Comedies.[41]

The mimes also pleased audiences by dancing, juggling, and doing acrobatics.

The mime performances were at first very informal. They took place in town squares and other random locations, so they were an early kind of street theater. In time, when they were written down, the mimes became slightly more formal and some were eventually presented in theaters. One of the first known writers to create a play from mime skits was Epicharmus, a contemporary of Aeschylus, born about 530 B.C. in a Greek town in Italy. Epicharmus introduced stock comic characters such as drunks, country bumpkins, and swaggering soldiers, strongly influencing later comic writers. None of his works have survived, but a small fragment of his play *Hope or Wealth* contains a speech by his most famous stock character—the parasite, or constant freeloader. "I dine with whoever wishes," the parasite proclaims. "He need only to invite me; yes, and with the man who doesn't wish—no need of invitation."[42] The parasite and other characters Epicharmus created became standard features of the Old Comedy, as well as of later Greek and Roman comedy.

Sometime in the late sixth century B.C., the Old Comedy, drawing on the phallic satyr processions and plays, the Doric mimes, and other more obscure sources, began to take shape. At first, comedies were not allowed in the City Dionysia. Satyr-plays were presented, but these continued to be connected with the tragedies they lampooned and were not considered separate formal comedies. It was not until 501 B.C. that comedies with their own stories and characters became a part of the drama festival of Athens. Official recognition of comedy—consisting of government money and competition for prizes— did not come until 487. The winner of the first comedy contest was the playwright Chionides, of whom almost nothing is known.

An Incredible Mixture of Comic Elements

The Old Comedy's most creative period was from about 450 to 404 B.C. This was the time when the Athenian empire was wealthiest and the demand for entertainment in the City Dionysia and other similar festivals was greatest. It was also the golden age of Athenian democracy. Citizens had complete freedom to speak out, even against the government, and politics and city leaders provided handy targets for comic playwrights to satirize, or poke fun at. Indeed, freedom of expression was perhaps the key element that made the wild style of the comedies of the time possible. James Butler writes:

> In Old Comedy, there was a degree of freedom and frankness—a license in language, situations, and stage portrayal—difficult for us to realize fully,

even today. It contained an incredible mixture of high [intellectual] and low [bawdy] comedy, satire, buffoonery, slapstick, verbal play . . . abuse, sex, caricature [making fun of people's looks and personalities] . . . singing, dancing, nudity, and vulgarity often in its crudest form.[43]

Typical of this vulgar humor was the frequent use of phalluses, a carryover from the satyr processions and plays. It was not unusual in these rowdy burlesques for actors, even those representing female characters, to parade around the stage wearing oversized phallic symbols.

Music was another important element in the Old Comedies. The chorus, which in comedy numbered twenty-four, was most involved in musical interludes. As Lionel Casson observes, these plays were

> more like our musicals than our [regular] comedies: they contained set pieces [musical numbers] which the chorus sang and danced. . . . When the chorus engaged in dialogue with an actor, its leader delivered the lines by himself, and in ordinary speech . . . but the whole body could, at any moment, break into brief bursts of song.[44]

Such combinations of silly and obscene skits and musical numbers could be and often were lacking in general structure, theme, and artistic merit. Yet in the hands of a few talented playwrights, the comic form attained a praiseworthy status and level of excellence. Unfortunately, the plays of comedy's first three masters no longer exist. These artists are known mainly from tiny surviving fragments of their works and from brief mentions of them in the works of other writers.

Cratinus supposedly produced about twenty-one comedies, of which nine won first prizes in the contests. He is also credited with developing the art of political satire, often using humor to attack the policies of Pericles and other politicians. Crates, another of the early masters, reportedly began as an actor in the plays of Cratinus. Crates went on to write eight plays of his own and to win three first prizes. His play *The Beasts* is said to have featured talking animals in the chorus.

Comic playwright Eupolis gained considerable fame for his fourteen plays, among them *The Flatterers* and *The Demes* [townships], and seven contest victories.

Master of the Comic Stage

Undoubtedly influenced by the early writers of Old Comedy just named, Aristophanes, who lived from about 445 to 388

A modern and somewhat fanciful depiction of a scene from Aristophanes' Birds. *It is doubtful that the original version featured the central arch and painted backdrop.*

A Forgotten Master

In this excerpt from his book Greek Comedy, *scholar Gilbert Norwood tells what little is now known about Eupolis, once widely renowned and awarded for his comic plays.*

"Eupolis, son of Sosipolis, was born in Athens in 445 B.C. and produced his first play in the course of his seventeenth year; that is, in 429 B.C. . . . That his life was short cannot be doubted. Various stories of his death, however untrue in detail, agree in placing it before the close of the Peloponnesian War (404 B.C.). . . . Eupolis was invariably placed beside Cratinus and Aristophanes as one of the . . . masters of Old Comedy; he won seven first prizes in his brief career; with *The Flatterers* he defeated Aristophanes's *Peace* in 421 B.C. Platonius [a later ancient writer] writes: 'Eupolis shows magnificent imagination in his plots. His opening scenes are great, and he excites in the play itself that imagination which other poets stir in the *parabasis* [choral song], being powerful enough to bring up figures of legislators from the dead, and through their mouths to advocate the passing or repeal of laws. This loftiness is matched by his charm and the aptness of his jests.' "

B.C., became the undisputed master of the Old Comedy. Scholar Moses Hadas states:

> In all, forty-four plays were attributed to Aristophanes. . . . The fact that the eleven plays [of his] which we have are the only complete specimens of Old Comedy to survive is sufficient proof that his work was esteemed the best. Five of the eleven plays . . . *Acharnians, Knights, Clouds, Wasps,* and *Peace*—were produced one each year from 425 to 421. Then followed the *Birds,* Aristophanes's acknowledged masterpiece, 414; *Lysistrata* and *Thesmophoriazusae,* 411; and *Frogs,* 405.[45]

Throughout his career, Aristophanes used biting satire to poke fun at the leaders and institutions of his day. "In a very real sense," says Lionel Casson,

> all of Aristophanes's plays are variations on three themes: politics and the [Peloponnesian] war with Sparta . . . literature . . . and education. . . . It can be seen immediately from this that practically every line he wrote was necessarily topical.[46]

The situations he depicted were usually fantastic and absurd. For instance, a common sausage maker outwits a respected city leader in *Knights.* The heroes of *Birds* attempt to build "Cuckoo City," a strife-free community in the sky, and a chorus of frogs croaks silly verses at the heroes of *Frogs.* Yet the parallels between these comedies and the real situations they were satirizing were perfectly clear to Athenian audiences. They understood that the author's exaggerations were a way of pointing out the real absurdities of specific people and events.

One of the best examples of Aristophanes' style in this respect is his depiction of war as an absurd and useless enterprise in *Lysistrata*, or "she who disbands armies." Tired of the seemingly ceaseless Peloponnesian War that has engulfed all of Greece, the title character organizes Greek women in a sex strike against the men. The women vow not to consent to sex until the men end their fighting. The women seize the Acropolis, and a group of old men (the younger ones being away in the war) attempt to retake it. The following exchange between the two groups, a mini-war satirizing the real one, is typical of the author's sharp, raw, and often violent humor:

> WOMEN: You villainous [bad] old men, what's this you do? No honest man, no pious man, could do such things as you.
>
> MEN: Ah ha, here's something most original, I have no doubt: a swarm of women-sentinels to man the walls without.
>
> WOMEN: So then we scare you, do we? Do we seem a fearful host [army]? You only see the smallest fraction mustered at this post.

Aristophanes and His "Happy Ideas"

Aristophanes' plays have a fairly consistent structure, as theater historian Oscar Brockett explains in this excerpt from History of the Theater.

"The plays are organized around a ruling theme, embodied in a rather farfetched 'happy idea' (such as a private peace with a warring power or a sex strike to bring an end to war). . . . A prologue establishes the mood and sets forth the 'happy idea'; the chorus enters, and there follows a debate (or *agon*) over the merits of the idea and a decision is made to try the scheme. A *parabasis* (or choral ode in which the audience is addressed directly) divides the play into two parts. In the *parabasis*, some social or political problem is often discussed and a line of action advocated. . . . The second part of the play shows, in a series of loosely connected scenes, the results of adopting the happy idea. The final scene (or *komos*) usually concludes with the reconciliation [settlement of differences] of all the characters and their exit to a feast or revels. These features of comic structure are sometimes rearranged but are almost always present."

In this scene from Aristophanes' Lysistrata, the title character resists her husband's advances.

MEN: Ho . . . shall we put a stop to all these chattering tricks? Suppose that now upon their backs we splintered these our sticks? . . . O hit them hard and hit again and hit until they run away, and perhaps they'll learn . . . not to have too much to say.

WOMEN: Come on then, do it! I won't budge, but . . . I'll snap till you can show no more than I myself beneath the lap. . . .

MEN: What vengeance can you take if with my fists your face I beat?

WOMEN: I'll rip you with my teeth and strew [throw] your entrails [insides] at your feet.[47]

The uproarious antics of Aristophanes and his contemporaries did not grace Athenian stages for long. Sparta's defeat of Athens in 404 B.C. temporarily ended Athenian democracy and threw the populace, including artists, into a state of despair and depression. Not only did playwrights lose much of their creative zeal, but the city's loss of prestige and wealth greatly reduced the number of *choregi* who could afford to back plays. For the most part, the comedies of the early fourth century B.C. were fewer, tamer, and less innovative. Yet the Old Comedy's legacy would remain a model for the comic writers of future generations and a reminder that the Greeks were the first people in the world to laugh at themselves.

Chapter

5 Much Ado About the Mundane: The New Comedy

The last important phase of ancient Greek theater occurred when Athens was no longer the political center of the Greek world. After its defeat at the end of the Peloponnesian War in 404 B.C., Athens became just another one of several city-states that vied for power and influence in an unstable and war-weary Greece. The way was open for a strong outside power to take advantage of Greek weakness. Philip II, king of Macedonia, in extreme north-

Alexander the Great of Macedonia brought Greek culture to the Mediterranean and the Middle East. His huge empire eventually broke up into several "Hellenistic" kingdoms.

ern Greece, grasped the opportunity and between 353 and 338 conquered his southern neighbors. His son, Alexander the Great, then embarked on a years-long military expedition that created a vast Greek empire stretching from Macedonia to India. In the process, Alexander spread Greek culture throughout the eastern Mediterranean and the Middle East. After he died, his empire split up into many independent Greek, or Hellenistic, kingdoms. So the two and a half centuries that followed, in which Greek ideas, language, and rulers dominated the areas conquered by Alexander, are usually referred to as the Hellenistic Age.

Hellenistic theater audiences were far more interested in comedy than in tragedy. Some tragedies, mainly those of Euripides and the other fifth-century masters, were still periodically performed. But the main emphasis in entertainment shifted away from serious themes to popular humor. In the drama of the period, now referred to as the "New Comedy," political satire, which had been the focus of the Old Comedy, was no longer the primary source of humor. The New Comedy emphasized realism. Most commonly, its humor derived from placing everyday people in realistic, though usually silly, social situations. In a way, then, this new brand of

This stone relief from a Hellenistic tomb shows actors holding masks of tragedy and comedy. The theater remained a popular attraction during this era.

comedy was the forerunner of modern situation comedies.

Everyday Stereotypes

The reasons for audiences' loss of interest in political satire will perhaps never fully be known. But it is likely that in the years directly following Athens's defeat, Aristophanes' style of political satire only reminded people of the city's problems: "People were in no mood to listen to the merciless criticism that had been the very soul of his greatest plays," Lionel Casson points out. "In their unhappy circumstances, Athenians wanted to be amused, not lectured."[48] In addition, the political climate often did not allow playwrights the freedom of expression they had once enjoyed. In the first decades of the fourth century B.C., Athenian democracy and freedom were at a low ebb. And the rulers

of the various Hellenistic kingdoms in which the New Comedy thrived were not usually tolerant of public criticism of themselves or their governments.

So the writers of the New Comedy shifted their focus to more mundane themes—most commonly, love, financial worries, and family relationships. And the plots increasingly came to revolve around the situations and problems of urban life. To a large degree, this shift in emphasis reflected the way the Greek world was changing. For a long time, Athens, with no more than 150,000 people living in its urban center, had been the only large Greek city. In Hellenistic times, by contrast, several larger and more prosperous cities rose in the eastern Mediterranean sphere. The largest and most influential were Alexandria, on the northern coast of Egypt, and Antioch, farther north along the coast of Syria, both with populations exceeding half a million. Because such urban centers became the focus of cultural life, the characters of the comedies were most often merchants and other city dwellers, or people visiting the city.

In contrast with the Old Comedy's inventive and varied plots and characters, those of the New Comedy were almost always repetitious and stereotypical. The same stock characters seemed to inhabit the same basic stories over and over again. According to James H. Butler:

> The most popular situations involve the exposure [leaving outside to die] of children at birth, the stealing of a young child, the seduction and violation of a young girl, and the final recognition of a long-lost daughter by those concerned so that marriage could take place. . . . A typical story for a New Comedy "potboiler" went something like this: A young man of good family, whose father is out of town on business, sets out to win the girl he loves. She is enslaved by a procuress [buyer and seller of prostitutes] who intends to sell her to the highest bidder. A boastful soldier is also competing for the girl. The young man calls

Someone Bring Me a Whip!

"DEMEAS (*exploding*) Parmeno, that's the end of you—you're lying to me!

PARMENO Who, me?

DEMEAS (*with ominous calm*) You see, Parmeno, I know the whole story. . . . I know that you know it too. . . .

PARMENO (*blustering*) Who says so?

DEMEAS Don't worry, I know it. Just tell me this—I'm right, yes? (*steps toward him menacingly*)

PARMENO (*cringing*) Yes—but we kept it secret—

DEMEAS (*roaring*) Secret! (*shouting to the servants in the house*) Inside there! Someone bring me a whip for this godforsaken slave of mine.

PARMENO Oh, no! Oh, god, no!

DEMEAS (*between his teeth*) So help me, I'm going to skin you alive.

PARMENO Skin me alive?

DEMEAS (*as a slave comes out and hands him a whip*) Right now.

PARMENO (*to himself, agonized*) I'm a goner! (*Whirls around and takes off, stage left*)

DEMEAS (*shouting after him*) Hey you! Where are you going, you good-for-nothing!"

upon his intriguing slave and an old bachelor friend of his father's for help. There is much intrigue and confusion. Finally, the young man frees the girl, learns that she is the long-lost daughter of a good family who was stolen in infancy, and a marriage follows.[49]

Exactly why Hellenistic audiences did not quickly tire of seeing the same plots repeated so often remains unclear.

Characters and Actors

In keeping with its use of everyday situations and characters, the New Comedy presented stories more realistically than had been done in the Old Comedy. Therefore, New Comedy playwrights dispensed with the interesting but unrealistic use of the chorus to highlight themes and actions. The new comic plays had no choral songs and no interaction between chorus and main characters. All the dialogue and verse parts were spoken or recited in regular speech. The chorus was reduced to a group of actors who entered periodically and sang and danced numbers that had nothing to do with the plots. In this way, the chorus functioned as a kind of curtain or between-acts entertainment. The emphasis on realism also eliminated most use of the oversized phallus, and only a few minor characters wore phallic symbols.

Although the New Comedy focused most of its attention on the characters rather than the plots, these characters were almost always presented in the same ways. Stock characters such as ardent young lovers, angry fathers, clever slaves, long-winded cooks, and self-important soldiers abounded. And the masks and costumes the actors wore allowed audiences to recognize the characters at a glance. As Marion Geisinger explains:

> While the costuming of the actors in the New Comedy more closely resembled the clothing of everyday life than it had in the earlier comic theater, the New Comedy employed the convention of always garbing [dressing] certain stock characters in certain colors. One such stock character was a roguish slave who always wore a white tunic and a very distinctive mask with red hair. Old men also wore white, but these oldsters were always clean-shaven and had closely cropped hair. . . . Young men wore purple; parasites were garbed in black or grey; and old women were presented in yellow or light blue. A courtesan [prostitute] was easily recognized, since that char-

acter always had her hair bound up with golden ornaments and brightly colored bands.[50]

The New Comedy's emphasis of characters over plot also greatly elevated the social status of the performers. In the fifth century, the playwrights had been the theater's principal stars. But in Hellenistic times, the contests among actors at the dramatic festivals came to overshadow those of the writers. As a consequence, theater folk became increasingly specialized and professional. To promote and protect their interests, they formed guilds, early versions of craft unions. The first, largest, and best known of these organizations was called the Artists of Dionysus. Oscar Brockett comments:

> Although the date of the guild's formation is uncertain, it was clearly in existence by 277 B.C. . . . The Artists of Dionysus included among its members poets . . . actors . . . members of the chorus, trainers, musicians, and costumers—all the personnel needed to produce plays. . . . As the name of the guild suggests, the performers retained their connection with Dionysus, even though they produced plays and acted at some non-Dionysian festivals.[51]

Hellenistic Theaters

As actors gained in prominence, the design of theaters changed to reflect their increased importance. In Hellenistic theaters, the *skene* moved forward, reducing the circular orchestra area into a semicircle. The front of the *skene* became a high raised stage, or *proskenion*, constructed of

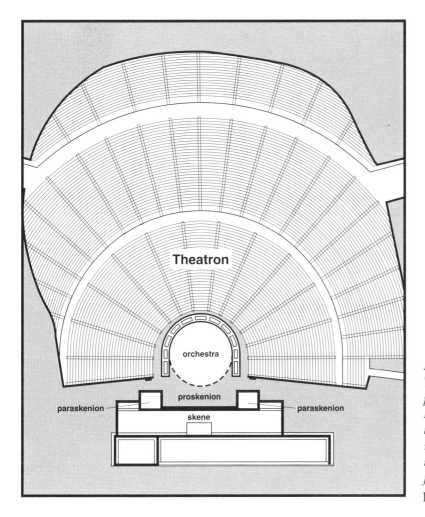

Theatron

orchestra

proskenion

paraskenion   paraskenion

skene

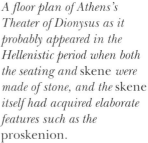

A floor plan of Athens's Theater of Dionysus as it probably appeared in the Hellenistic period when both the seating and skene *were made of stone, and the* skene *itself had acquired elaborate features such as the* proskenion.

wood or stone. It varied in height from 8 to 12 feet and in width from about 45 to 140 feet. On this stage, the actors were more prominent than ever before. They made their entrances and exits mostly through doors and other openings in the back of the stage. Supporting the *proskenion* was a row of columns, between which painted screens, called *pinakes*, could be inserted to suggest changing locales. Another kind of painted scenery consisted of wooden triangular prisms, the *periaktoi*, located near the stage's far sides, or wings. To suggest a new locale, a stagehand rotat-

ed the *periaktoi*, revealing a different scene painted on each side.

These changes in classical theater design became standard in the late fourth century. Older theaters, such as that of Epidauros, were converted to accommodate the raised stage and other new features. And newer theaters generally followed the model of the first important dramatic arena built in Hellenistic times, the Theater of Priene, located near the Greek town of Ephesus on the coast of Asia Minor. Built about 330 B.C., the Priene theater had a stage 9 feet high and

Two Greek theaters in Asia Minor: the huge Theater of Ephesus, which sat 25,000 (top), and the Theater of Priene, the first important Hellenistic theater.

65 feet wide, and sat about 6,000 people. Some Hellenistic theaters were much larger. The Theater of Megalopolis in southern Greece had seating for 21,000, and the Theater of Ephesus, not far from the Priene building, sat 25,000.

In these and hundreds of other theaters that dotted the Greek kingdoms of the eastern Mediterranean, audiences delighted in the works of many popular comic playwrights. Among the best known were Diphilus, Philemon, and Philippides, who wrote during the late fourth and early third centuries B.C. Although collectively the three men wrote more than two hundred comedies, only fragments of these, consisting of fewer than a hundred lines each, survive.

A Profound but Puzzling Legacy

By far the most popular and influential playwright of the New Comedy was Menander, who lived from about 342 to 293 B.C. Of his 108 comedies, only one complete manuscript, that of *The Grouch*, has survived. About half each of *The Arbitration*, *The Shorn Woman*, and *The Woman*

Menander: Charm and Theatrical Triumph

This excerpt from Moralia (*quoted in* Gilbert Norwood's Greek Comedy) *by the first century A.D. Greek-Roman writer Plutarch illustrates the remarkably high regard in which ancient critics held Menander and his New Comedy plays.*

"The style of Menander shows so uniform a polish, such a harmonious blend of manner, that while it traverses a wide range of emotion and character, adapting itself to all shades of personality, its unity is apparent, its individuality unimpaired. . . . There have been many renowned craftsmen, but no workman ever made a shoe, no theatrical artist a mask, no costumer a garment, that fitted equally well man and woman, child, elder and slave; yet Menander has so blent [blended] his diction [dialogue] that it suits every character, every rank, every age; and that though he was still a youth when he laid hand to the work and died at the zenith of his poetical and theatrical skill. . . . Menander's charm makes him utterly satisfying, for in these works that present with universal appeal the splendors of Greece, society finds its culture, the schools their study, the theater its triumph. The nature and possibilities of literary elegance were by him revealed for the first time: he has invaded every quarter of the world with his invincible glamor, bringing all ears, all hearts, under the sway of the Greek language. What sound reason for entering a theater does the cultivated man ever find, except Menander?"

of Samos, as well as hundreds of fragments from other plays, have also survived. Menander was extremely well liked, not only in his own time, but also in later ages. The Romans in particular considered him the best Greek playwright, and his works profoundly influenced Roman drama. The later Greco-Roman historian Plutarch said of Menander:

There have been many renowned craftsmen, but no workman ever made a shoe, no theatrical artist a mask, no costumer a garment, that fitted equally well man and woman, child, elder and slave. . . . What sound reason for entering a theater does the cultivated man ever find, except Menander?[52]

And the Roman writer Quintilian exclaimed, "O Menander and life! Which of you has copied the other?"[53]

These and other high praises for Menander have puzzled many modern theater historians and critics. The surviving pieces of his work show little evidence

Menander (ca.342-ca.293 B.C.) was considered the master of the New Comedy.

tertaining. Typical of his characters and situations were plots in which clever slaves stuck their noses in their masters' business and feared getting caught and punished. Evidently, ancient audiences found cringing servants particularly funny. For example, in *The Arbitration*, the slave Onesimus worries about his master's wrath, saying:

> He keeps shouting these awful things about himself, he's all worked up, his eyes are bloodshot—I'm scared. I'm scared stiff. In his condition, if he sees me . . . he's liable to kill me. That's why I sneaked out of the house. But where am I going to go? What am I going to do? I'm a goner, I'm sunk! . . . He's coming out now. God in heaven help me—if you can![55]

As far as scholars can tell, almost all Menander's works and those of his New Comedy colleagues featured slaves who meddled in their masters' affairs and suffered the consequences.

Yet despite its repetitive themes and characters and relative tameness in comparison to the Old Comedy, the New Comedy lasted much longer. Greek audiences flocked to theaters to see Menander's plays long after the playwright's death. And beginning in the mid-third century B.C., some of the spectators at these performances were visiting Romans, who much admired Greek theater. No one realized at the time that Roman armies and navies would soon sweep out of Italy and eclipse the waning power of the Greek kingdoms. In the process, Rome would absorb much Greek culture, and the New Comedy's characters and plots would find new life on Roman stages.

of great craftsmanship and are certainly far less innovative than those of Aristophanes. Indeed, asks Lionel Casson, "How could [Menander] have achieved such a towering reputation when his plots and characters were so limited . . . his stock in trade . . . basically the same romantic stuff that made up so much of Greek New Comedy?"[54] Perhaps Menander's fame rested on his happening to do the right thing at the right time. It is likely that the later Greeks and the Romans particularly liked the New Comedy's brand of situation humor, which Menander served up better than anyone else.

Menander's plays may not have been great literature, but existing excerpts show that they were certainly amusing and en-

6 Variety and Vulgarity: Early Roman Theater

After Greek civilization declined in the latter part of the Hellenistic Age, the Romans carried on many of the theatrical traditions the Greeks had created. The Romans, who used the Latin language, were a highly industrious and practical people who first inhabited west-central Italy between 1000 and 750 B.C. In the late sixth century, they set up the Roman Republic, consisting of an assembly of citizens who made laws and chose administrators to run the state, and a senate composed of well-to-do landowners who advised the administrators. In the next few centuries, the Romans expanded outward from central Italy. They conquered neighboring peoples, including the Greeks, who had heavily colonized southern Italy between the eighth and sixth centuries B.C. By 265 B.C., the Romans had completely unified the Italian peninsula under Rome's national symbol—the eagle.

A Remarkable Gift for Borrowing

For the most part, the early Romans had no theatrical traditions of their own. This was mainly because they were not particularly inventive, especially regarding artis-

tic and literary themes and ideas. "A sense of poetry was not strong in the Roman people," comments Edith Hamilton in her classic book *The Roman Way to*

A Roman senator addresses his colleagues. The Romans borrowed most of their theatrical traditions from the Greeks.

Western Civilization. "Their natural genius did not urge them on to artistic expression."[56] As late as 280 B.C., when they were fighting the Greek city-states of southern Italy, the Romans still had no formal theatrical institutions. "There were no 'cultivated' audiences," says Sheldon Cheney.

> The Romans of the time were hardheaded, materialistic, unimaginative fighters, with the admirable qualities of courage, enterprise, and a sense of integrity and justice . . . but with no taste for . . . the arts, none for personal refinements.[57]

The Romans' natural genius lay in their remarkable ability to borrow ideas from other peoples and to adapt these to their own special needs. And of all the cultures they encountered, they most admired and borrowed from the Greeks. Even before conquering the Greeks in Italy, the Romans, perhaps without realizing it, absorbed many Greek cultural ideas that had earlier spread throughout the Italian peninsula. Among these concepts were early forms of theatrical entertainment, the Roman versions of which eventually became extremely popular among Romans of all walks of life. "The result," explains theater historian Allardyce Nicoll, "is that the Roman theater was built out of what the Greeks created, and the Latin plays were based confessedly on [Greek] models."[58]

Etruscan Influences

The only notable theatrical entertainments the Romans enjoyed before they began borrowing from the Greeks were simple, informal poems known as "Fescennine verses." And even these were not native to Rome. The adaptive Romans borrowed them from the Etruscans, a people who, before being conquered by Rome in the fourth century B.C., inhabited the fertile region known as Etruria, located immediately north of Rome. Etruscan culture strongly influenced that of Rome. For example, the famous "Roman" arch used in construction was really an Etruscan idea that the Romans adopted.

The Etruscans recited and sang the Fescinnine verses at a variety of religious and social celebrations. According to James H. Butler, the verses

> grew out of rural festive occasions celebrating successful harvests and were especially given at the feast of Silvanus, an old Italian divinity and protector of fields, gardens, and cattle. They were also popular at weddings, for it was thought that they helped to avert misfortune. The crude, improvised verses were delivered [spoken or sung] in meter [to a set rhythm], often sung in a most suggestive and graphic manner, and hurled back and forth by the performers, much to the delight of those watching.[59]

We do not know exactly when the Romans began using these verses in Latin at their own celebrations. It may have been as early as the sixth century B.C. What is more certain is that by the mid-fourth century B.C., young Romans often performed Etruscan songs and dances at religious and social ceremonies. The performers, called *histriones*, improvised their own dialogue and gestures to accompany the singing and dancing. The modern term

Rome's Debt to the Etruscans

In his widely read book, History of the Theater, *Oscar G. Brockett explains how Etruscan culture influenced Roman religious festivals, in which theatrical farces and mimes were presented.*

"Before the direct Greek influences on Rome, Etruria was the dominant influence on Roman theatrical activities, although it is difficult to assess the culture's contributions fully since so few written records have survived from Etruscan civilization. Nevertheless, it was probably from Etruria that Rome inherited many features of its religious festivals. . . . Sacred festivals in Etruria included acting, dancing, flute playing, juggling, prizefighting, horseracing . . . and competitive sports. . . . Some Etruscan festivals were held in conjunction with fairs to which people came from faraway places. All these attributes help to explain the nature of Roman festivals, which mingled diverse activities in an atmosphere partly religious, partly secular, even carnival-like. Other Etruscan practices also probably influenced Roman theater. Among these was the use of music, dance, and masks in almost all Etruscan ceremonies; music was especially important, for it accompanied activities ranging from sacrifices to boxing matches to daily work."

An Etruscan bronze figure of a discus thrower. Etruscan festivals influenced the development of Roman theater.

Though the Romans were prolific builders, constructing roads, aqueducts, and arches like the one pictured here, they did not build permanent stone theaters until the first century B.C.

"histrionic," referring to actors and their gestures, comes from this Latin word. Possibly the *histriones* resembled vaudeville and movie "song-and-dance men" of the early twentieth century—Al Jolson and George Burns, for example—who improvised remarks and jokes between and during musical numbers.

The Popular Farces

By the late fourth century B.C., another form of theatrical entertainment had become popular in Roman towns and villages. This was the *fabula Atellana*, or "Atellan farce." A farce is a comic play that utilizes slapstick humor and improbable situations. Apparently, the Romans got the idea for these entertainments from the Greeks of southern Italy. As early as the sixth century, the Greeks performed improvised street farces known as *phylakes*, in which actors wearing masks clowned around, told jokes, sang, and danced. Eventually, Roman versions of the *phylakes* became popular in the region directly south of Rome, where the performers spoke Oscan, the local Italian dialect. As the farces spread throughout Italy, they were done in Latin.

The Atellan farces were not full-fledged plays; they were more like the comic sketches one might see on a TV variety show like *Saturday Night Live*. Each of these short, largely improvised pieces revolved around a simple everyday idea or situation, such as getting drunk, overeating, or shoplifting. As in the Greek *phylakes*, the actors wore masks. They also portrayed stock characters. As historian J.P.V.D. Balsdon explains:

> The parts were as traditional as in a Punch and Judy show: two different buffoons, Maccus, the glutton [one who eats too much], and Bucco, whose mask had inflated cheeks; Pappus, the old gaffer [fuddy-duddy], in whose person all the follies and comic afflictions of old age were mocked; and Dossenus, the hunch-back, butt for the many [jokes] which could be

levelled at . . . schoolmasters, philosophers and others.[60]

Eventually, perhaps beginning in the first century B.C., authors wrote down many of the most popular farces. But all that has survived of these are some titles, such as *Maccus the Soldier, The Bride of Pappus, The She-Goat, The Baker,* and *The Pregnant Virgin.* Scholars have pieced together most of what is known about the farces from scenes painted on Roman vases and craters, or jars. Margarete Bieber, an expert on these artifacts, describes one of the farcical scenes depicted:

Theft, such as that of fruit and wine, had already been a theme in the old

[Greek] farce. Money, cake, wine, and meat are stolen in the Italian farce. The most delightful and realistic scene is presented to us by the crater of Assteas [a fourth-century painter of vases]. . . . The old man Charinus has thrown himself upon his money chest. . . . Two thieves try to tear him away. The one, named Cosilus, has taken hold of his left arm. . . . The other, named Gymnilos, pulls with both hands at his left foot and thigh. Between them, they will roll him off the chest and get the money.[61]

Apparently, an actual performance of this farce consisted of the two thieves sneaking

Winning in Love

In The History of the Greek and Roman Theater, *scholar Margarete Bieber describes how paintings on many ancient Roman vases and kraters, or bowls, depict scenes from popular comic farces. Here she tells about the use, in the farces, of contrasting love themes—one involving masters, the other slaves.*

"Generally . . . it is the young man who wins in love. When age and youth, probably even father and son, fight over a woman, as on a [k]rater in Ruvo [an Italian town known for its fine vases], the woman will naturally fall to the young man. Both men, wielding swords in their right hands, have grasped the woman with their left hands. The youth, however, has a firm grip on her wrist and also has put his foot on her foot. The old man has only her shawl in his hand. Thus, in the next moment the youth will pull up the woman and run off with her while the father will be left standing with the empty [shawl]. . . . A crater in the Moscow Museum depicts two slaves, who instead of quarreling over a woman as the masters do, are satisfied with one big girl for the two of them. They lead her along carrying big bolsters [pillows] in richly-ornamented covers of the kind used for couches at banquets. . . . The departure for a gay banquet is a popular and fitting conclusion for any comedy or farce."

This stone relief from the famous Roman town of Pompeii shows actors wearing traditional grotesque masks performing a comedy.

up on the old man, fighting with him over the money, and making off with it. As the old man whined and complained about his loss, the audience roared with laughter.

Roman Burlesque

Although the Atellan farces were widely popular, the Romans were even more fond of another form of comic entertainment they borrowed from the Greeks—the mime. The Doric mimes of mainland Greece had made their way into the Greek cities in Italy at least by the fifth century B.C. And when the Romans conquered and absorbed these cities in the early third century, they encountered and adopted the mimes.

The Roman mimes differed from the Greek versions in two important ways. First, Roman women often performed as mimes, something never seen in Greece. This was undoubtedly a reflection of the higher social status women enjoyed in Rome. Second, Roman mimes did not wear masks. Instead, they used their own facial expressions for comic effect, which gave their performances a realistic touch. This convention and other aspects of realism, such as earthy, often sexually obscene, lines and gestures, set the mimes apart from the Atellan farces.

Another difference between the two genres was that the mimes also featured jugglers and acrobats, who likely recited vulgar jokes during their acts. Sometimes the performers exhibited near or total nudity. According to noted scholar Jane F. Gardner, "It was customary at mime performances . . . to make loud demands for the [female mimes] to 'take them off' and for the women to comply and strip."[62] Thus, in many ways, the mimes were like early twentieth-century American burlesque shows, which featured a variety of acts, including slapstick sketches, stand-up comics, dancers, jugglers, and strippers. The Roman mime shows "mirrored the low life of the times," comments Marion Geisinger, who adds:

> Certain stock types were developed: there was the fat, talkative fool, the stupid rustic fool, and the foolish old man, to name but a few. These easily recognizable characters were por-

trayed by mimes both male and female, who usually improvised dialogue to fill out standard plot situations. . . . The mimes were so well received that in time they became the principal features of [everyday Roman] entertainment. The chief reason for their success was the intensely human quality contained in their vulgarity.[63]

Indeed, the Roman mimes were so successful that in the late third century B.C. they became the featured attraction of the *Ludi Florales*, a festive holiday celebrated from April 28 to May 3.

A Fickle Public

It is important to note that the increase in the mimes' popularity was not accompanied

In another depiction of a theatrical comedy from Pompeii, the master of the house (with staff) lectures his slave (left) and his daughter.

by a decrease in the popularity of other forms of entertainment. In Greece, new theatrical styles tended largely to replace older ones. For example, the heyday of tragedy and Old Comedy faded as the New Comedy became popular. In Rome, by contrast, Atellan farces and other kinds of entertainment remained popular right alongside mimes. And these forms, in turn, remained popular later when full-length plays appeared. The Romans loved and demanded a variety of theatrical styles. As Oscar Brockett puts it:

> We can probably grasp the essence of Roman theater more readily by comparing it with United States television programming, for it encompassed acrobatics, trained animals, jugglers, athletic events, music and dance, dramatic skits, short farces, and full-length dramas. The Roman public was as fickle [changeable] as our own: like channel-switchers, they frequently left one event for another and demanded diversions capable of withstanding all competition.[64]

Greek theater would continue to be the main source of these diversions. In the late third and early second centuries B.C. the Romans would finally begin to write full-fledged plays and perform them on stages. And the models for many of these works, constituting the first important examples of Roman literature, would come directly from still another Greek comic style—the New Comedy.

Chapter

7 Nothing New Under the Sun: Late Republican Drama

In the third, second, and first centuries B.C., the Roman Republic's efficient military machine moved outward from Italy and, like an unstoppable wave, engulfed the entire Mediterranean world. Among the many nations the Romans conquered were the Hellenistic kingdoms. At first Roman travelers, and later Roman soldiers, spent months and often years in Greek cities. The degree of Roman exposure to Greek language, customs, and other aspects of Greek culture was far more intense than it had been earlier with the Greek cities in Italy. The result was a new and powerful surge of Roman interest in Greek civilization.

The imitative Romans were quick to absorb many aspects of the Greek culture they so admired, including theatrical styles and conventions. For years, the Romans had delighted in the comic antics of the Greek-inspired Atellan farces and mimes. These short, informal, and largely unstructured skits had been the Romans' only theatrical tradition. Now, as Rome's empire enfolded the Greek world, Roman soldiers, travelers, and traders witnessed firsthand the glories of full-length Greek plays, impressively staged in authentic Greek theaters. These presentations included both revivals of the great fifth-century tragedies and performances of the currently trendy New Comedies of Menander and his colleagues.

Greatly inspired by Greek theater, about 240 B.C. the Romans began presenting their own versions, in Latin, of popular Greek plays. This was the beginning of a golden age of Roman theater, which produced some of Rome's finest writers and plays. Because it encompassed the final two centuries of the republic, this theatrical period is often referred to as "late republican drama."

The First Theaters and Plays

The first performances of full-length Roman plays based on Greek models took place at one of Rome's most important religious festivals—the *Ludi Romani*. This oldest of Roman holidays was celebrated in September in honor of Jupiter, the Roman version of the Greek Zeus, king of the gods. The plays were so popular that in the following fifty years five other important festivals introduced formal theatrical presentations.

Permanent Roman theaters did not yet exist. So the actors performed on makeshift wooden stages that could be erected in less than a day. Likely set up in

Roman Actresses

In this excerpt from Women in Roman Law and Society, *classical scholar Jane F. Gardner describes Roman women performers in general and one actress in particular.*

"Women singers, dancers, and musicians [in ancient Rome] are known, performing both on public occasions and at private functions. They provided a cabaret [floor show] at the livelier Roman dinner parties. . . . The dancing girls from Spain, and specifically those from Cadiz [a Spanish city], were famous. . . . Women did not appear on the 'legitimate' stage, but only as mime-actresses. . . . Those performers known to us by name were slaves or freedwomen [slaves granted their freedom], with names usually of Greek origin. Some of these seem to have been more or less appropriate stage names, such as Eucharis, 'charm,' Paizusa, 'playful.' Eucharis, already a freedwoman when she died at the age of 14 in the late Republic, was commemorated by her . . . father who praises her education and training 'as if at the hand of the Muses [goddesses of the arts]' and represents her as saying: 'I graced the games of the nobles with my dancing and first appeared before the common people in a Greek play [mime].' "

front of the temple of the god a particular festival honored, these platforms copied the design of raised Hellenistic stages. The Roman stages were perhaps 5 to 8 feet high and up to 60 feet wide. They were backed by a wooden wall about 12 feet high called the *scaenae frons*. This wall featured doors for the actors' entrances and exits and probably painted scenes representing the fronts of houses, stores, barns, or other plot locales. Together, the wooden stage and *scaenae frons* probably looked much like the *proskenion* of Hellenistic theaters such as that at Priene.

The first artist credited with translating and producing Greek plays on these early Roman stages was Livius Andronicus, a Greek who became a Roman citizen. His adaptations of Greek originals were the first, or at least among the first, of those presented at the *Ludi Romani* in 240 B.C. Little is known about Andronicus, and none of his adaptations have survived. But he was very popular in his own time, and his work apparently strongly influenced other writers. One of these playwrights, Gnaeus Naevius, who lived from about 270 to 201 B.C., was Rome's first important native dramatist. About Naevius, James H. Butler comments:

All evidence about him bears out the fact that he showed a great deal of originality as well as independence in his writing. . . . One of his earliest plays, if not his earliest, was given at the public games in Rome, probably the *Ludi Romani* in 235 B.C. The remains of his work today consist of the titles of seven of the nine tragedies he wrote, 34 titles of his comedies, and 190 lines and fragments.[65]

Naevius also wrote some historical plays based on both myths and real events from Rome's past. For instance, his work *Romulus* dealt with the exploits of the title character, one of Rome's legendary founders. But historical plays proved unpopular with Roman theatergoers and few were written after Naevius's time.

Enjoying a bit more popularity in the early years of Rome's golden age of drama were tragedies, their plots mostly derived from those of the Greek tragedians. Yet these serious literary pieces did not achieve the widespread appeal they had enjoyed in Athens's golden age. It is not clear why the Romans did not take to tragedy, as the Greeks had. But simple demographics—the average Roman was far less literate and educated than the average Greek—was undoubtedly a factor. Appreciating tragedy's complicated plots and lofty poetry probably required a degree of culture and sophistication most Romans lacked. Whatever the reasons, few playwrights produced tragedies. As Oscar Brockett points out:

> The names of only three tragic writers between 200 and 75 B.C. are now known: Quintus Ennius (239-169), Marcus Pacuvius (ca. 220-ca. 130), and Lucius Accius (170-ca. 86). It is difficult to generalize about this early tragedy, since no plays survive. Judging from fragments, titles, and contemporary comments, however, the majority of the plays were adapted from Greek originals . . . while a smaller number were based on Roman subjects. . . . They probably did not depart structurally in any important way from Greek tragedies.[66]

In this scene from the early Roman tragedy Hercules and Madman, *a character prepares to cast an infant onto a flaming funeral pyre.*

Greek Characters and Conventions

By far the most popular plays presented in Rome in the golden age were comedies based on Greek New Comedy. Although the actors in the Roman versions spoke Latin, the plots were usually rehashes or modifications of Greek originals. Even the locales and character names used in the Roman comedies were Greek. Evidently, the playwrights set their stories in Greece to avoid Roman censors. According to Edith Hamilton:

> It was of great practical importance for a Roman comedian to choose a far country for his fun. The stage has always been a most attractive field for legislators, and the Romans . . . revelled in . . . censorship. A law . . . condemned people to be whipped who wrote anything defamatory [that insulted important people], and [a playwright] had been imprisoned and then exiled . . . for writing a play in which there was a single disrespectful [mention] of dignitaries. . . . Faced with this dilemma . . . the comedians sensibly turned to foreign parts for their scenery.[67]

Roman comedy writers quickly learned that disguising as Greeks those they wanted to insult was the way to avoid the whipping post.

The Roman comedies also borrowed many of Greek comedy's conventions, including that of men playing women's roles. For the most part, mime remained the only theatrical genre in which Roman women were allowed to take part. Greek stock characters also populated Roman

A second-century A.D. stone engraving shows Roman slaves. Most Roman families owned slaves, who performed nearly all of society's menial labors.

stages. Bragging soldiers, parasites, stupid old men, and prostitutes were some of the most common types. None was featured as frequently, however, as the clever slave, who achieved even more popularity in Roman than in Greek theaters. Nearly every Roman family had at least one slave. Slaves did almost all the labor that kept society moving, and many slaves, in particular Greeks who came to Rome as war captives, were better educated than most free Romans. It is no wonder that the slave was so often depicted in drama. "No Roman comedy could be written without him," says Edith Hamilton. "In every play he is the chief personage [character], the only one with brains, who succeeds in fooling all of the people all of the time."[68]

One Greek convention ignored by theatrical producers and actors during Roman drama's golden age was the use of masks. Roman actors used their own facial expressions to show character, mood, and emotion. This custom may have developed partly because mimes, Roman society's most popular theatrical performers, did not wear masks. The custom likely also stemmed from the changing acting styles. Each Roman actor played a single character per play, in contrast to Greek actors, who often played two or more. So Roman actors had the opportunity to develop and perfect their characters to a high degree, in many cases becoming well known and in demand for such expertise. They probably felt that hiding their faces behind masks severely limited the range of emotions their characters could portray.

Master of Nonstop Gags

While some actors gained fame and drew audiences to Roman theaters, a few playwrights earned formidable reputations of their own. In particular, two writers—Plautus and Terence—were very famous in

---

A Roman "Broadway Producer"

In Masters of Ancient Comedy, *Lionel Casson explains the general manner of lining up Roman plays and hiring acting troupes during the second century B.C.*

"In Plautus's time there were at least four annual festivals whose programs included drama, and special events such as the funerals of great men or victory celebrations provided still further opportunities for a playwright. On none of these occasions were plays featured, as in Greece. They were offered as just one more item on a bill of fare of popular entertainment: the Roman officials who ran the festivals simply hired a theatrical troupe along with the required number of gladiators, boxers, wrestlers . . . and so on. The troupes, small groups of five or six actors, generally of Greek extraction, were managed by a *dominus gregis*, or "leader of the troupe," who entered into a contract with the appropriate officials to supply a given number of plays. . . . It was the job of the *dominus* to find scripts for his troupe to put on. He either bought them himself or recommended their purchase by the officials. Plautus was, therefore, in much the same position as a dramatist of today. He had to peddle his plays to the Roman equivalent of a Broadway producer."

Plautus (ca.254-ca.184 B.C.) was a master of gags, puns, and other slapstick humor.

interesting for the holiday audiences of Rome. . . . It is said that he composed one hundred and thirty plays. . . . Of this number we have twenty.[69]

Among the best-known of these surviving works are *The Pot of Gold*, about an old miser who fears someone will steal his treasure; *Miles Gloriosus* (or *The Braggart Warrior*), which shows a swaggering, womanizing soldier to be a fool; and *The Twin Menaechmi*, a tale of twins separated at birth and later reunited under confusing and humorous circumstances. Other notable plays by Plautus include *Amphitryon*, *The Comedy of Asses*, and *The Haunted House*.

Although Plautus borrowed many of his plots and stock characters from the New Comedy, his presentation was fresh and often inventive. And to Menander's rather mild brand of humor he added many openly slapstick and often bawdy situations and jokes. In fact, Plautus's jokes were not only funny and appealing, but also almost nonstop, designed to please the average city dweller who came to see his plays. Says Lionel Casson:

> To Plautus, the play was not the thing; the audience was. The customers were rude Romans who had come to laugh from the belly, and he did his level best to accommodate them. He had no hesitation in interrupting the flow of the action at any point for a scene of pure slapstick or for a series of jokes. . . . At all costs he kept the pot of the action boiling, the stream of gags and puns . . . flowing swiftly and steadily.[70]

Typical of such gags were those in which the clever slave got away with insulting or

their own time and are now considered the undisputed masters of Roman comedy. Titus Maccius Plautus lived from about 254 to 184 B.C. As scholar Kevin Guinagh tells it:

> [Plautus] got his start by working about the theater. He is supposed to have been a stage carpenter, many of whom must have been needed since the theaters were impermanent and had to be built and torn down for each festival. . . . A man of education and great native ability, he was able to take the plays of the writers of the New Greek Comedy, among others Philemon and Menander, and make them

dominating his master, who was usually somewhat slow-witted. In *The Haunted House*, for example, the slave Tranio tries to tell his master Theopropides something important.

> TRANIO: He said the corpse of the murdered man came to him in a dream—
>
> THEOPROPIDES: (*interrupting, with relief*) Then it was just a dream?
>
> TRANIO: That's right. But listen. He said that this corpse told him that this is the way—

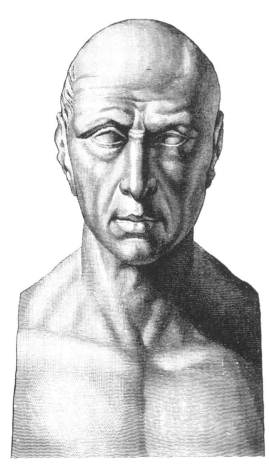

Terence (185-159 B.C.) often defended himself and his ideas in the prologues of his plays.

> THEOPROPIDES: (*interrupting incredulously*) In a dream?
>
> TRANIO: (*impatiently*) What was it supposed to do? Come around and chat in broad daylight? It was a corpse, dead for sixty years! (*Disgustedly*) Sometimes, you're pretty stupid, Theopropides.
>
> THEOPROPIDES: (*meekly*) All right, I'll keep quiet.[71]

Plautus was also adept at character humor. Often, a character's own words or mannerisms made him look silly and humorous while he continued to take himself seriously, as in the conceited soldier's opening speech in *Miles Gloriosus*:

> See that my shield be polished so that its sheen is more resplendent than the noon-day sun. When the battle is joined, it must dazzle the eyes of the fierce ranks of the enemy before me. But ah! my sword: how doleful and sad is its spirit, lamenting its long disuse! How eagerly it pines to make havoc of my foes![72]

Nothing New Under the Sun

Plautus's successor as master of Roman comedy—Publius Terentius Afer, known to history as Terence—lived from about 185 to 159 B.C. Born a slave in northern Africa, he was brought to Rome as a child by a well-to-do Roman senator. His master educated and later freed him, and Terence became a member of Rome's upper-class literary circle, which included well-known poets and playwrights. In his short lifetime, he wrote only six plays, all of which have survived. They are *Andria*, roduced in 166, *Mother-in-Law* (165), *Self-Tormentor* (163), *Eunuch* (161), *Phormio* (161), and *The Brothers* (160).

Terence aimed his humor more at the educated upper classes than at the less sophisticated middle and lower classes Plautus had played to. So Terence's plays contained little slapstick and few rowdy situations and jokes. While Plautus had used such comic devices liberally to spice up the plots he had pirated from the Greek playwrights, Terence's works were much truer adaptations of the Greek originals. Terence made no excuses for copying the Greeks, especially Menander. In fact, he felt the more closely a new work retained the "purity" of the Greek original, the better that work was. Anyway, said Terence, coining a now famous phrase, "There's nothing new under the sun; everything one says has been said before."[73]

Please Be Good Enough to Pay Attention

Yet while his plots were not original, Terence produced much admirable dialogue and verse, and his adaptations had a charming style of their own. As Lionel Casson points out, "The language and verse in which he clothed what he borrowed are among the best things Latin literature has to offer."[74] The charm of Terence's style is apparent in the prologue, or introductory speech, of *Phormio*, in which the author addressed the audience directly, saying:

> Now, what I really have to tell you is this—and please listen. I have a new play for you. In Greek it's called *He Who Goes to Court*, but your author has titled his Latin version *Phormio*, since a scrounger [roaming adventurer] by that name has the leading role and triggers most of the action—as you'll see if you'll do the author the favor of hearing it through. Please be good enough to listen in silence and pay attention. I don't want to have happen what happened once before when, because of a disturbance, our company had to leave the stage—a stage we've returned to only because of the efforts of our leading man and the aid of your generosity and good will.[75]

The kind of disturbance Terence referred to was becoming increasingly common in his time. During the first performance of his play *Mother-in-Law*, the audience walked out because of a rumor that boxers and rope dancers were performing nearby. And in the middle of the second staging of the play, the spectators hurried away to witness gladiators fighting to the death. Terence and his colleagues had no inkling that these episodes foreshadowed the end of Rome's golden age of drama. The ever-changing moods and tastes of the Roman masses would soon sweep traditional comedies and tragedies from the stage.

Chapter

8 Theater in the Roman Empire: Art or Immorality?

In the century following the triumphs of Plautus and Terence, the nature of Roman entertainment changed in response to sweeping political and social changes. In the first century B.C., Rome was wracked by bloody civil wars as powerful military generals vied for control of the state. After much death and strife, in the final decades of the century the republic fell and gave way to the Roman Empire. The new Rome was in effect a dictatorship in which the common people had few rights or privileges.

From the beginning, the Roman emperors recognized that the key to maintaining their power was effective control of the masses. Because slaves did much of the everyday work, a majority of Romans, both rich and poor, had a great deal of leisure time. And this, the emperors realized,

In this modern engraving of a Roman street scene, citizens converse at one of the entrances to a stone theater. The mother and child have just been dropped off by the horse-drawn "taxi" at right.

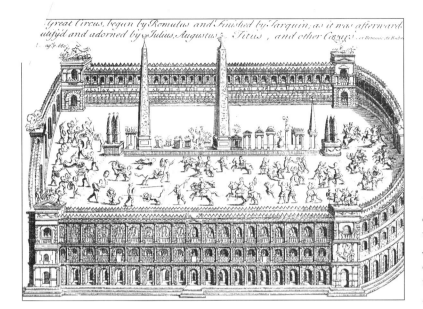

The Circus Maximus, known as the "Great Circus," in which chariot races and other spectacles were staged, was over 2,000 feet long, 700 feet wide, and sat more than 250,000 people.

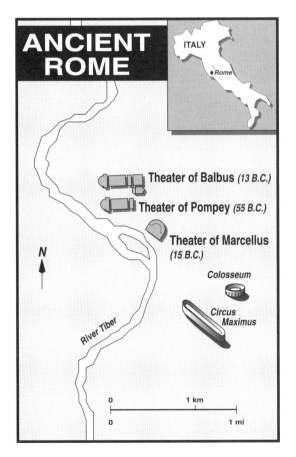

posed a potential danger to the state. An idle, discontented "mob," as the leaders usually referred to the Roman masses, could prove unruly and might even rebel.

Bread and Circuses

So the emperors adopted a twofold strategy to keep the masses occupied and content. The government distributed free handouts of bread and grain and also sponsored large-scale daily entertainments, including gladiatorial combats and chariot races, in big arenas called circuses. Under this policy of "bread and circuses," the Roman people increasingly came to expect and desire varied, exciting, and spectacular forms of entertainment. They also became more impatient and harder to please. Just as audiences had left performances of Terence's plays to see rope dancers and gladiators, spectators of the Roman Empire often "shopped around" for the most colorful and thrilling show.

Exhibitions in which men, and sometimes women, fought to the death, wild animals tore each other to shreds, and full-sized ships fought mock battles in flooded stadiums became commonplace.

Compared with such spectacles, traditional comedies and tragedies must have seemed tame. And in fact, by the end of the first century B.C., theatrical producers saw the demand for plays with careful plotting, dialogue, and characterization dwindle. "It was not that the comedies of Plautus, Terence, [and] the tragedies of Ennius, Naevius, [and others] . . . lacked merit or were unappreciated," scholar F.R. Cowell explains. "They simply could not compete with the rival forms of entertainment which made a stronger appeal to the Roman mob."[76]

In place of traditional plays, producers offered cheaper, more colorful, and often more vulgar forms of entertainment. Mimes, which had always been cheap and vulgar, remained popular, as did the Atellan farces. And pantomimes, stage presentations that used elaborate dancing and music to tell stories, also became popular theater fare.

Permanent Theaters

None of these theatrical shows could have competed at all with the gladiators and charioteers had Rome's theaters remained makeshift temporary wooden structures. The fights and races were staged in stone

Rome's Largest Theater

In The Theater and Drama of Greece and Rome, *scholar James H. Butler describes the Theater of Marcellus, erected by the emperor Augustus in 11* B.C.

"It seated approximately 14,000, making it the largest of [Rome's] three permanent stone theaters. The reconstructed ground plan indicates that the vaulted side passageways between the stage (*pulpitum*) and the first tier of seats served as entranceways to the lower tier of seats. Above these were the *tribunalia* [seats reserved for government officials]. Other seats in the theater could be reached by the central passageway (*praecinctio*) and radiating stairways, or by stairways and tunnels under the seating areas opening into these areas by *vomitoria* [entrances]. A colonnaded [column-lined] gallery was located at the top of the *cavea* [seating area]. Storerooms on each side of the stage, a scene building directly behind the *scaenae frons*, and a rear terrace and portico [roofed walkway] completed this theater complex."

The ruins of Rome's Theater of Marcellus, which Augustus Caesar, the first Roman emperor, erected in the year 11 B.C.

stadiums with permanent seating for thousands. They were often equipped with bathrooms, restaurants, awnings to protect spectators from the sun, and other comforts. Attempting to compete with these buildings, in the first half of the first century B.C. some wealthy Romans erected extremely elaborate temporary theaters, some filled with statues and colorful decorations.

The need for more permanent theaters soon became clear, and in 55 B.C., under the leadership of the powerful general Gnaeus Pompeius Magnus, known as Pompey, the state built Rome's first stone theater. Called the Theater of Pompey after its benefactor, it sat about 8,000 people. Its stage, or *pulpitum*, was made of stone covered by tiles and was likely raised

about five feet above the semicircular orchestra area. The *scaenae frons* behind the stage was also of stone and decorated with columns, statues, and gold ornaments.

The Theater of Pompey proved a popular attraction, and the government soon erected two more theaters. The Theater of Balbous, with seating for about 8,000 people, opened in 13 B.C. And the Theater of Marcellus, which sat some 14,000, was built by Augustus, the first Roman emperor, two years later. In the two centuries that followed, the Romans built about 125 more theaters around the empire. Nearly all had similar structural features, along with standard comforts such as awnings to block the sun, vendors selling fast food and cushions, and showers to allow patrons to cool themselves on hot days. These theaters also had two other distinguishing features that evolved from the earlier wooden versions. Says Oscar Brockett:

> First, some time between 133 and 56 B.C., a curtain was introduced in the Roman theater. It was dropped into a slot in the front of the stage at the beginning of a performance and was raised at the end. Second, the Roman stage had a roof, which served at least two functions: it protected the elaborate *scaenae frons* from the weather, and it improved the acoustics [bounced the actors' voices toward the audience].[77]

The behavior of the audiences that frequented these elegant theaters was something less than elegant. According to James H. Butler, Roman theater audiences

> were a noisy, restless, boisterous, rude lot, more often interested in *who* was present *in* the theater than in *what* was happening *on* the stage. . . . The only reserved seats . . . were those provided for senators. . . . This must have meant a mad scramble for good seats. All classes went to the theater—men, women, children, and slaves. . . . Claques (hired applauders) were hired by actor-manager-playwrights to gain audience support. . . . If successful, playwrights and actors were in a better position to increase their fees.[78]

The Rewards of Acting

Indeed, for the actors applause and money were often the only rewards available in an otherwise thankless profession. In Greece, actors had been respected and even honored. But for reasons that are unclear, as a rule Roman actors were admired only while onstage. Offstage, their status was barely higher than that of beggars and criminals. Many were slaves or former slaves, in general giving the profession a low-class image, and nearly all carried the label of *infamia*, or "social outcast." There

This fourth-century Roman scene, constructed of mosaic tiles, depicts masked actors performing a farce or mime.

were notable exceptions, of course. A few performers became respected "stars" who counted senators and even emperors as their friends. During late republican times, for example, the actor Roscius earned a stellar reputation and hobnobbed with the rich and famous, including the great orator-legislator Cicero. And in the empire years, the mimes Favor and Latimus received lavish praise and personal favors from the emperors Vespasian and Domitian, respectively. However, such exceptions remained just that. The majority of actors, comments James Allen,

> were despised and denounced as moral lepers, outcasts from society. Long after the breaking up of the Empire this attitude . . . persisted. Indeed . . . the prejudice which still exists in certain circles toward the acting profession harks back to the days of Rome.[79]

With little chance of social acceptance, then, actors sought as a reward for their work the highest fees they could command. Apparently, most were paid by the performance, a standard fee for a common mime during the empire being about 500 sesterces. The value of this sum by today's standards is difficult to calculate. But with it a Roman in the first century A.D. could rent a small but comfortable room in the city for perhaps a few weeks or more. So an average actor's pay must have been more than adequate to live on, assuming he or she did not squander the money. As is still the case today, the most successful performers earned a great deal more than the average. As J.P.V.D. Balsdon states:

> We hear of a *mima* [mime] who earned 200,000 *sesterces* a year in the late Republic. . . . Roscius earned over half a million *sesterces* a year. His contempo-

---

An All-Embracing Art

In his second-century A.D. work, Dialogue on Dancers (*quoted here from Oscar G. Brockett's* History of the Theater)*, the Greek writer Lucian of Samosata describes the Roman pantomimes of his time.*

"Other entertainments of eye or ear are but manifestations [displays] of a single art. . . . The pantomime is all-embracing. . . . The performer's art is as much intellectual as physical: there is meaning in his movements; every gesture has its significance. . . . He must be a critic of poetry and song, capable of discerning good music and rejecting bad. . . . So potent is his art that the licentious [sexually immoral] spectator is cured of his infirmity by seeing the evil effects of passion, and he who enters the theater in sorrow leaves it serenely. . . . [However] pantomimes cannot all be artists; there are ignorant performers who badly bungle their work."

rary Aesopus [another renowned actor] was worth twenty millions when he died. Good actors, in fact, made more money than playwrights, who normally sold their copyright [right to produce a play] to a producer outright. Terence sold the *Eunuch* in the second century B.C. for a mere 8,000 *sesterces.*[80]

From Sword-Swallowers to Ballet Dancers

In the empire, Roman actors had a number of different theatrical media in which to perform and earn their money. A few became known for their work in the "tragic recitations"—small-scale performances, usually in imperial palaces or palatial private homes, attended by the privileged and the well-to-do. The recitations began in the first century A.D. after theaters had ceased to present tragedies. The actors, probably wearing costumes and masks, recited scenes from well-known Greek and Roman tragedies. The emperor Nero, who reigned from 54 to 68, was especially fond of the recitations and, fancying himself a gifted actor, even performed some himself.

For the most part, however, the chief theatrical forms, those that entertained the masses, remained the farces and mimes. To ensure continued popularity with audiences who preferred and demanded colorful, spectacular, and offbeat entertainment, the mimes increased both their variety and their vulgarity. A typical mime performance in the empire consisted of much more than bawdy comic sketches, jugglers, and acrobats. Mimes also offered stilt-walkers, sword-swallowers, fire-eaters, magicians, mind-readers, for-

The emperor Nero, who reportedly considered himself a talented actor and musician, sometimes performed in public.

tune-tellers, and performing animals. Thus, Roman mimes were the direct ancestors of modern carnivals and circuses.

Almost as popular as the mimes was the *fabula saltica*, or pantomime. Introduced in the early years of the empire, this form of entertainment remained widely popular among Romans of all classes for several centuries. More artistic and dignified than the mimes, the pantomimes were stories told through dance—the forerunners of modern ballet. Usually, pantomimes were performed by a solo dancer. Male performers were most common, but a few women also took part. The plots were usually taken from mythology or history, and the dancing was accompanied by

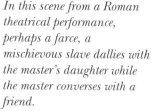
In this scene from a Roman theatrical performance, perhaps a farce, a mischievous slave dallies with the master's daughter while the master converses with a friend.

a chorus singing a narration and an orchestra of flutes, cymbals, and other instruments. According to James Allen:

> The single dancer (*pantomimus*) represented the various characters, both male and female, as well as the plot, by the movements of the body. The illusion was usually enhanced, indeed, by change of costume and mask, but the success of the performance depended mainly on the skill of the pantomime in portraying character and suggesting situation.[81]

Some pantomime actors developed the art to a high level of perfection and earned both large fees and critical acclaim. Writing in the first century A.D., the Roman scholar Quintilian said of pantomimes:

> Their hands demand and promise, they summon and dismiss; they translate horror, fear, joy, sorrow, hesitation, confession, repentance, restraint, abandonment, time, and number.

They excite and they calm. They implore and they approve. They possess a power of imitation which replaces words. To suggest illness, they imitate the doctor feeling the patient's pulse; to indicate music they spread their fingers in the fashion of a lyre [harp].[82]

The Death of Ancient Theater

In time, however, such high praises for theatrical performances became increasingly scarce. Farces, mimes, and pantomimes remained widely popular well into the fourth century. But in the mid-to-late years of the same century, Christianity gained ascendancy in Roman politics and society. The emperor Constantine, who reigned from 324 to 337, tolerated the Christians, who had earlier been hated and persecuted. He even converted to the faith on his deathbed. Afterward, the sect grew in numbers and influence, and in 378 the emperor Theodosius made Christianity the state religion and forbade the worship of the traditional Roman gods in temples.

Traditional theatrical forms also suffered under the Christians. According to Oscar Brockett:

> The theater was a favorite target of the Christians for at least three reasons. First, it was associated with the festivals of pagan [non-Christian] gods. Second, the licentiousness [sexual immorality] of the mimes offended the moral sense of the church leaders. Third, the mimes often ridiculed such Christian practices as baptism and the sacrament of bread and wine. As a result, the break between church and theater was inevitable.[83]

According to legend, on the eve of battle Constantine saw a vision of a cross surrounded by the words, "With this sign, you will conquer."

Devils from the Theater

In his work On the Public Shows (*quoted here from Edmund Fuller's* A Pageant of the Theater), *the Roman Christian writer Tertullian warned about what could happen to people who simply attended the theater.*

"Why, may not such men be in danger of devils entering into them? For the case has happened, the Lord is witness, of that woman who went to the theater, and returned from it with a devil. When the unclean spirit, in the exorcism [act of driving the devil from the body], was hard pressed because he had dared to attack a believer, he boldly said, 'and most righteously I did it, for I found her in my own place [the theater].' It is well known, also, that there was shown to another in her sleep, on the night of the day in which she had heard a tragedian, a linen cloth [on which the tragedian's name was written, presumably by God], and that this woman, at the end of five days, was no longer in the world."

An engraving shows barbarians burning and sacking Rome.

In 398, church leaders threatened to excommunicate, or banish from the church, any Christian who attended the theater on a church holy day. And actors were forbidden to receive church sacraments such as baptism unless they first gave up their profession. In his work *On the Public Shows,* the Roman Christian writer Tertullian summed up the church's view that the theater was immoral and indecent. He called actors "victims of public lust" and described the theater as "a stronghold of every vice [sin]" and "a private chamber of immodesty in which nothing is approved except that which elsewhere is disapproved."[84]

Despite such condemnations, it was not the church, but instead politics and economics, that finally killed Roman theater. Non-Christians, of whom there were still many, continued to attend the theater in the fifth century. But during these same years hordes of Germans, Franks, and other nomadic peoples from central Europe—in Roman eyes "the barbarians"—repeatedly invaded the empire and sacked Rome. They drove the last Roman emperor from the throne in 476, the year usually denoted as the "fall of Rome." In reality, the invaders were hardly barbaric, since their leaders continued to support the theater for several more decades and even restored the decaying Theater of Pompey.

But the Roman world, once so efficient in its institutions, government, and social organization, was also decaying. In a single generation, Rome sank from the world's most prosperous city, a metropolis of a million souls, to a near-ghost town in which a mere 20,000 people scrambled to feed and clothe themselves. Much of the vast Roman Empire broke up into small, disorganized, and culturally backward European kingdoms. In addition, the empire's magnificent roads, stadiums, and temples began to crumble because the leaders of these lesser realms lacked the money, the will, and the know-how to keep them in repair.

The theaters began to crumble too, for no more public money flowed into the arts and no wealthy *choregi* were left to back plays. The last recorded performance in a Roman theater occurred in 533. After that, the magnificent 900-year theatrical legacy of the Greeks and Romans—from the grand poetry of Aeschylus to the comic wit of Plautus and Terence—faded into the obscurity from which it had sprung. The theater was now a memory, but one that refused to die. It would sleep for long centuries, waiting patiently for those with a poet's spirit to come along and rediscover it.

Chapter

9 To All People in All Ages: The Legacy of Ancient Theater

The influence of ancient theater on modern entertainment has been profound. Nearly all of today's theatrical conventions, from acting styles and costumes to scenery and the shape of stages, originated with the Greeks and Romans. Yet the impact of the old theater on the new was not a sudden and widespread phenomenon. The modern world's absorption of ancient theater's splendid legacy was instead a very gradual and uneven process.

For centuries after Rome's power in Europe faded, the plays of the Greek and Roman playwrights were largely ignored. In medieval times, the period of roughly eight hundred years following the fall of Rome, the classical civilizations of Greece and Rome became an increasingly distant memory. The remains of the ancients' temples, bridges, and other structures dotted Europe. For the most part, these decaying ruins had become objects of idle curiosity or easy sources of materials with which to build newer, cruder structures. Among the ancient and crumbling artifacts were the magnificent stone theaters, where masked comics and tragedians had given life to the words of great writers. Now the stages and bleachers stood empty, mute testimony of a glorious past.

As the ancient plays gathered dust on forgotten shelves, new dramatic forms

evolved. Most of these were religious plays staged in churches in the European kingdoms that had risen from the wreckage of the Roman Empire. Among these realms were England, France, Spanish Navarre, and Italian Tuscany. The religious plays were reenactments of biblical stories, many depicting episodes from the life of Jesus of Nazareth. They were usually intended to glorify God rather than to entertain, and they bore little or no resemblance to formal ancient theater.

Europe's Roving Minstrels

Yet, though the ancient theaters were silent, the traditions of the old playwrights, producers, and actors lingered. From generation to generation after Rome's fall, individual performers passed on these traditions to others. No longer able to perform plays in theaters, many of the Roman mimes and other actors took to the road. Some singly, and others in troupes, they wandered through European countrysides, singing, dancing, or performing tricks for anyone who would toss them a few pennies. In time, these wandering "minstrels" became a regular feature of medieval life, and people in

A group of minstrels gathers in medieval England, perhaps to perform at a wealthy wedding or important state function.

the famed "court jesters." Meanwhile the roving troupes continued their treks, occasionally coming together in huge groups for special occasions. At the wedding of England's Princess Margaret in 1290, for example, 426 minstrels performed.

Many minstrel troupes continued to perform as medieval times gave way to the Renaissance of the fourteenth, fifteenth,

A medieval court jester, whose outfit is a modified version of a Roman mime's costume.

villages and castles looked forward to their periodic visits. Says Marion Geisinger:

> Wherever they stayed, wandering minstrels were usually made very welcome. To the great houses and castles of the nobility they had virtually a free right of entry, for in addition to providing entertainment, the minstrels brought with them news of foreign parts—news which they no doubt carefully colored to suit each particular audience. Sometimes, indeed, an itinerant [traveling] minstrel would please some king or noble so well that he would settle down permanently in his service.[85]

The minstrels who stayed on in the palaces of the European nobility became

Two commedia dell'arte actors cavort and gesture wildly. The comic sketches they performed were the direct descendants of those presented in Greek and Roman farces.

and sixteenth centuries. During this period, much of Europe underwent a cultural awakening as literature, painting, sculpture, architecture, and other arts reached high levels of excellence. Many of the finest ideas and achievements of the Renaissance originated in Italy. There, in the sixteenth century, arose a popular form of theatrical entertainment known as the commedia dell'arte: traditional minstrel troupes who performed, as they had for centuries, in castles, village squares, and local festivals and fairs.

The commedia actors performed little playlets, in essence comic sketches. Marion Geisinger states:

Typically the stories were farces. . . . Subjects were mistaken identity, avarice [greed], the conflict between old husbands and young wives. . . . [T]he preeminent theme was marital infidelity [cheating on husband or wife]. Young wives of old men and virtuous daughters of rich merchants engaged in involved and complicated love intrigues. The valets and servant-maids engineered the innumerable ridiculous situations . . . so that there was a continual interplay of plot and counter plot.[86]

That the commedia plots, jokes, and characters resembled those of Roman comedies was no accident. Indeed, the commedia actors based their work directly on the plays of Plautus, Terence, and Menander. Europe's wandering minstrels had managed to keep the main elements of ancient theater alive and viable for more than a thousand years. The commedia's stock characters were nothing more than slightly updated versions of ancient originals. Among them were Harlequin, the clever servant who liked playing pranks; Pantalone, an aging and naive merchant who was often the butt of Harlequin's jokes; the Captain, a braggart soldier; and Pierrot, a sad and simple-minded servant. Many other elements of commedia performances, especially sight gags, came from ancient theater. For example, the character Pantalone often wore a mock phallus for comic effect.

Ancient Humor's Unbroken Chain

The commedia had an immediate and long-lasting effect on European theater. It reached France in the 1570s and became so popular that some commedia troupes eventually began performing in the small wooden theaters of the day. In the mid-1600s, a gifted French playwright, Jean-Baptiste Poquelin, known simply as Molière, fell in love with the commedia's plots and characters. His now classic comedies are filled with characters and situations inspired by the commedia dell'arte. Among them are *Tartuffe*, produced in 1664, *The Doctor in Spite of Himself* (1666),

The French playwright Molière (1622-1673) glorified the comic antics of the commedia characters.

A scene from Molière's The Imaginary Invalid, *a farce about a hypochondriac, a healthy person who only imagines himself to be ill.*

and *The Imaginary Invalid* (1673). Molière, in turn, inspired countless other comic writers and performers in the following centuries.

The commedia's characters and humor also served as the basis for traveling puppet shows, which became standard entertainment in European town squares and festivals from the 1600s on. When they reached England, they came to be called "Punch and Judy" shows after the commedia stock character Pulchinella. "Punch" was the direct descendant of the Roman stock character Maccus, the glutton of the Atellan farces.

Meanwhile, other minstrels and traveling entertainers kept the traditions of the ancient mimes alive. Eventually, English and American burlesque, performed in theaters in the early 1900s, inherited that special ancient mix of comedy, singing, dancing, slapstick, juggling, and nudity. Many of modern burlesque's top comics—

such as Charlie Chaplin and the Marx Brothers—and song-and-dance men—such as Al Jolson—went on to become popular film stars. They introduced the ancient routines to new generations. Television variety and comedy shows, in turn, did the same. At the same time, carnivals and circuses, also direct descendants of ancient mime, became popular modern forms of entertainment worldwide. Thus can be seen a nearly unbroken chain of popular theatrical conventions and humor stretching from ancient times to the present. It began with the classic Greek and Roman farces and mimes, and moved through the ages via the minstrel shows, the commedia dell'arte, the circuses, the burlesque theaters, and finally movies and TV.

Resurrected Riches

Yet the influence of the ancient plays, mimes, and farces on later popular entertainment constitutes only a part of Greek and Roman theater's modern impact. The ancient plays and theaters themselves, so long ignored, eventually enjoyed an unprecedented rediscovery and revival. In fact, the rediscovery in the 1400s and 1500s of classical civilization's cultural glories was one of the driving forces behind the European Renaissance. Suddenly, people saw the ancient ruins in a new light. Greek and Roman literature, sculpture, and architecture became the rage in wealthy and educated circles all across Europe. Artists openly copied the ancient styles, and scholars scrambled to unearth whatever classical manuscripts they could find. What had been seen for so long as dust-covered refuse was now literary gold.

Among the resurrected riches were the surviving plays of Plautus and Terence. Revivals of these works began in Italy, where printed editions appeared in the 1470s. According to Margarete Bieber:

> The Pot of Gold was presented in 1484 in the palace of the Quirinal [residence of Italian kings]. The Twin Menaechmi was performed before the Pope in the Vatican in 1502. . . . At the wedding of Lucrezia Borgia [an Italian noblewoman] at Ferrara [in northern Italy] in 1502 five comedies of Plautus were presented on five succeeding days. In the sixteenth century many comedies were produced in Italy which combined the motifs [themes and styles] of Latin comedies with portrayal of contemporary Italian life.[87]

Similar revivals rapidly spread across Europe. And contemporary writers were quick to borrow the plots of these comic works. William Shakespeare's *Comedy of Errors*, for instance, is an updated version of Plautus's *Twin Menaechmi*. And *The Miser*, by Molière, is a thinly veiled version of *The Pot of Gold*, also by Plautus.

Meanwhile, many of the ancient tragedies also enjoyed rebirth and revival. By the mid-1500s, scholars had translated a number of the Greek and Roman tragedies, and wealthy art patrons paid to mount splendid productions of them. Sophocles' mighty work *Oedipus the King* was among the first. Its modern theatrical life, reports classical scholar Charles R. Walker, began

> in Vicenza [Italy] on March 3, 1585, when the Sophoclean tragedy was performed amid much pomp at the opening of the famous Theater Olympico

of [the great Renaissance architect Andrea] Palladio. The play was presented in an admirable translation by the Venetian scholar and statesman Orsatto Giustiniani. . . . "It was fitting," wrote Filippo Pigafetta, a member of the first audience, "that this most renowned theater in the world should have as its first presentation the most excellent tragedy in the world."[88]

New Art Forms and Theaters

Such attempts to stage the ancient masterpieces soon stimulated the creation of new theatrical art forms and the theaters to house them. In the late 1500s, members of the respected Camerata Academy in Florence, Italy, set the lofty goal of performing the Greek tragedies in their original form. The scholars knew from studying descriptions in old manuscripts that the plays of Aeschylus and Sophocles had featured a chorus. Research also suggested that the works had used music and dance and that part of the dialogue had been sung. The Camerata scholars wrote music and songs they hoped would give the tragedies an authentic feeling. And in the process they invented modern opera.

The new theatrical form featured lead actors singing solo songs called arias. The actors also performed recitative by chanting their regular dialogue to musical accompaniment. The chorus sang its lines, too, sometimes in a dialogue with the actors. Opera was almost instantly popular among Europe's educated classes, and artists soon began writing their own original versions. The most successful themes and stories came from mythology and his-

A nineteenth-century audience watches a Punch and Judy puppet show, with characters and situations based on ancient Roman originals.

tory. Opera's phenomenal popularity is illustrated by its growth in a single city. In 1637, Venice, Italy, had only one opera house. By 1700, it had eleven, which had produced a total of more than 360 operas.

Wealthy Europeans also began building theaters in which to stage both the ancient plays and the new operas. For their design, they were inspired by the first-century B.C. Roman architect Vitruvius. His manuscript describing Hellenistic and Roman theaters had been unearthed in 1414 and printed in 1486. According to Margarete Bieber:

Italian designers followed [Vitruvius's] . . . plans for arranging the auditorium, the orchestra, and the stage. Their experiments in reproducing the Roman theatrical forms culminated in the Theater Olympico in Vicenza, designed by Palladio and erected 1580-1584. The auditorium and orchestra have the Roman semi-circular arrangement. . . . In the Farnese Theater at Parma [Italy] built in 1618 the Roman forms are distorted. The auditorium is elongated . . . and a kind of *scaenae frons* architecture is added above the seats. This led to our modern theaters with boxes [with seats] arranged around the auditorium in several stories.[89]

From Ancient to Modern Stages

In a sense, the revival of classical drama that began in the Renaissance never ended. The theatrical plays and forms of the Greeks and Romans became the accepted models of great theater and have been performed and copied ever since. The twentieth century has seen many productions of the classic plays presented by college theaters. One of the most ambitious, mounted in 1954 at Randolph-Macon College, in Lynchburg, Virginia, featured all three plays in Aeschylus's Oresteia trilogy in the original Greek. Professional troupes have staged their own successful versions. Laurence Olivier, widely regarded as the greatest actor of the century, earned critical acclaim for his portrayal of Oedipus in *Oedipus the King* at London's Old Vic Theater in 1945. And veteran actor-director John Gielgud staged a now-famous production of Euripides' *Medea* on Broadway in New York City in 1947.

Adaptations of the classics also frequently appeared on Broadway. Shakespeare's version of Plautus's *Twin Menaechmi* became the musical comedy *The Boys from Syracuse* in 1938. And in 1962, composer Stephen Sondheim adapted several of Plautus's plays in the hit musical *A Funny Thing Happened on the Way to the Forum*. Onstage, and later in the film version of *Funny Thing*, comic actor Zero Mostel played the clever slave Pseudolus, who led

Actor Zero Mostel (right) portrays Pseudolus in the original Broadway production of A Funny Thing Happened on the Way to the Forum.

A Bloodcurdling and Haunting Scream

One of the most famous modern adaptations of Greek tragedy was Laurence Olivier's performance of the title role in Oedipus the King *in London in 1945. In his biography of the great actor, Anthony Holden describes how Olivier worked to make the character's suffering real.*

"It was an immensely powerful performance, moving from stark horror to affecting pathos [sadness] as the doomed monarch gradually discovers that he has unwittingly murdered his father and married his mother. At the awesome moment when this dark truth dawns, Olivier uttered a cry so bloodcurdling, so haunting, that many who were there insist they can still hear it today. Reaching, as so often, for one devastating physical effect to form a centerpiece for the performance . . . Olivier was looking for a sound which distilled [captured simply] the elusive concept [of fate]. 'Oh, Oh,' was all the script offered, which he had already transformed to a sound nearer 'Er' when he read in a magazine of the way ermine [white-furred weasels] are trapped in the Arctic: the hunters put salt on the ice, the ermine licks it and its tongue freezes to the ice. It was from the unique torment of the trapped ermine that Olivier conjured his devastating Oedipus scream. To him, the technique justified his belief that 'it is next to impossible to produce the effect of great suffering without the actor enduring some degree of it.'"

Laurence Olivier (1907-1989) as Sophocles' King Oedipus. In his long and distinguished career, the actor received numerous Oscars and other awards, as well as a British knighthood.

a cast of Roman stock characters through a series of hilarious escapades. The swaggering soldier was appropriately named Miles Gloriosus after the title of one of Plautus's famous plays.

The success of ancient tragedies and comedies on modern stages only can be explained by the talent and insight of their creators. The genius of Aeschylus and Sophocles, of Plautus and Terence, was that they were able to capture the essence of human feelings. They saw what made people cry and what made them laugh and translated these qualities into words for the actors to speak. That their works are fresh and appealing to audiences today proves that the feelings and emotions explored by the ancients are universal. In terms of the human spirit, Terence was right when he said, "There's nothing new under the sun." Echoing the old master was a line written for Pseudolus in *Funny Thing*, two thousand years later: "Old situations, new complications . . . something for everyone, a comedy tonight."[90] That same sentiment will, no doubt, be echoed again on stages two thousand years hence.

Notes

Introduction: The Poetry of Human Conflict

1. Aristotle, *Poetics,* in Robert Maynard Hutchins, ed., *The Works of Aristotle,* in *Great Books of the Western World Series.* Chicago: Encyclopaedia Britannica, 1952.

2. Eugene O'Neill Jr., Introduction to *The Complete Greek Drama,* Whitney J. Oates and Eugene O'Neill Jr., eds. New York: Random House, 1938.

3. Oscar G. Brockett, *History of the Theater.* Boston: Allyn & Bacon, 1982.

Chapter 1: Obscurity Gives Birth to Brilliance: The Origins of Theater

4. Lionel Casson, *Masters of Ancient Comedy.* New York: Macmillan, 1960.

5. Sheldon Cheney, *The Theater: Three Thousand Years of Drama, Acting, and Stagecraft.* New York: Tudor Publishing, 1939.

6. Brockett, *History of the Theater.*

7. Aeschylus, *The Suppliants,* in *The Complete Greek Drama.*

8. Aristotle, *Poetics,* in *The Works of Aristotle.*

9. Edmund Fuller, *A Pageant of the Theater.* New York: Thomas Y. Crowell, 1965.

10. Phyllis Hartnoll, *The Concise History of the Theater.* New York: Harry N. Abrams, 1968.

11. Marion Geisinger, *Plays, Players, and Playwrights: An Illustrated History of the Theater.* New York: Hart Publishing, 1971.

12. James H. Butler, *The Theater and Drama of Greece and Rome.* San Francisco: Chandler Publishing, 1972.

13. Geisinger, *Plays, Players, and Playwrights.*

14. Casson, *Masters of Ancient Comedy.*

Chapter 2: Gods from the Machine: Greek Theatrical Production

15. Anna Michailidou, *Knossus: A Complete Guide to the Palace of Minos.* Athens: Ekdotike Athenon, 1993.

16. James T. Allen, *Stage Antiquities of the Greeks and Romans and Their Influence.* New York: Cooper Square Publishers, 1963.

17. Butler, *The Theater and Drama of Greece and Rome.*

18. Brockett, *History of the Theater.*

19. Bernard M.W. Knox, "The Theater of Dionysus," in Sophocles, *Oedipus the King.* New York: Pocket Books, 1959.

20. Brockett, *History of the Theater.*

21. H.C. Baldry, *The Greek Tragic Theater.* New York: W.W. Norton, 1971.

22. Geisinger, *Plays, Players, and Playwrights.*

23. O'Neill, *The Complete Greek Drama.*

24. O'Neill, *The Complete Greek Drama.*

25. Butler, *The Theater and Drama of Greece and Rome.*

Chapter 3: Tragedy's Three Giants: The Golden Age of Greek Drama

26. Edith Hamilton, *The Greek Way to Western Civilization.* New York: New American Library, 1942.

27. Paul Roche, "The Message of Aeschulus," in *The Orestes Plays of Aeschulus.* New York: New American Library, 1962.

28. Hamilton, *The Greek Way.*

29. Aristotle, *Poetics,* in *The Works of Aristotle.*

30. Butler, *The Theater and Drama of Greece and Rome.*

31. Roche, *The Orestes Plays of Aeschulus.*

32. Aeschylus, *The Eumenides,* quoted in Allardyce Nicoll, *World Drama: From Aeschulus to*

Anouilh. New York: Harcourt, Brace and Company, 1949.

33. Knox, "The Theater of Dionysus."

34. Geisinger, *Plays, Players, and Playwrights.*

35. Sophocles, *Oedipus the King,* in C.A. Robinson, ed., *An Anthology of Greek Drama.* New York: Holt, Rinehart, and Winston, 1960.

36. Rex Warner, "Euripides and His Life," in *Three Great Plays of Euripides.* Translated by Rex Warner. New York: New American Library, 1958.

37. Euripides, *Medea,* quoted in *The Complete Greek Drama.*

Chapter 4: Poking Fun at Life's Absurdities: The Old Comedy

38. Aristotle, *Poetics,* in *The Works of Aristotle.*

39. Aristotle, *Poetics,* in *The Works of Aristotle.*

40. Cheney, *The Theater.*

41. Butler, *The Theater and Drama of Greece and Rome.*

42. Epicharmus, *Hope or Wealth,* quoted in Gilbert Norwood, *Greek Comedy.* New York: Hill and Wang, 1963.

43. Butler, *The Theater and Drama of Greece and Rome.*

44. Casson, *Masters of Ancient Comedy.*

45. Moses Hadas, "The Man, His Rivals, His Successors," in Moses Hadas, ed., *The Complete Plays of Aristophanes.* New York: Bantam Books, 1962.

46. Casson, *Masters of Ancient Comedy.*

47. Aristophanes, *Lysistrata,* in *The Complete Plays of Aristophanes.*

Chapter 5: Much Ado About the Mundane: The New Comedy

48. Casson, *Masters of Ancient Comedy.*

49. Butler, *The Theater and Drama of Greece and Rome.*

50. Geisinger, *Plays, Players, and Playwrights.*

51. Brockett, *History of the Theater.*

52. Plutarch, *Moralia,* quoted in Norwood, *Greek Comedy.*

53. Quintilian, *The Training of an Orator,* quoted in Casson, *Masters of Ancient Comedy.*

54. Casson, *Masters of Ancient Comedy.*

55. Menander, *The Arbitration,* quoted in Casson, *Masters of Ancient Comedy.*

Chapter 6: Variety and Vulgarity: Early Roman Theater

56. Edith Hamilton, *The Roman Way to Western Civilization.* New York: New American Library, 1932.

57. Cheney, *The Theater.*

58. Nicoll, *World Drama.*

59. Butler, *The Theater and Drama of Greece and Rome.*

60. J.P.V.D. Balsdon, *Life and Leisure in Ancient Rome.* New York: McGraw-Hill, 1969.

61. Margarete Bieber, *The History of the Greek and Roman Theater.* Princeton, NJ: Princeton University Press, 1961.

62. Jane F. Gardner, *Women in Roman Law and Society.* Indianapolis: Indiana University Press, 1991.

63. Geisinger, *Plays, Players, and Playwrights.*

64. Brockett, *History of the Theater.*

Chapter 7: Nothing New Under the Sun: Late Republican Drama

65. Butler, *The Theater and Drama of Greece and Rome.*

66. Brockett, *History of the Theater.*

67. Hamilton, *The Roman Way.*

68. Hamilton, *The Roman Way.*

69. Kevin Guinagh, "Plautus," in Kevin Guinagh and Alfred Paul Dorjahn, eds., *Latin Literature in Translation.* New York: Longmans, Green, and Company, 1952.

70. Casson, *Masters of Ancient Comedy.*

71. Plautus, *The Haunted House,* quoted in Casson, *Masters of Ancient Comedy.*

72. Plautus, *Miles Gloriosus*, quoted in Nicoll, *World Drama*.

73. Terence, quoted in Nicoll, *World Drama*.

74. Casson, *Masters of Ancient Comedy*.

75. Terence, *Phormio*, quoted in Casson, *Masters of Ancient Comedy*.

Chapter 8: Theater in the Roman Empire: Art or Immorality?

76. F.R. Cowell, *Life in Ancient Rome*. New York: G.P. Putnam's Sons, 1961.

77. Oscar G. Brockett, *The Theater: An Introduction*. New York: Holt, Rinehart, and Winston, 1969.

78. James Butler, *The Theater and Drama of Greece and Rome*.

79. Allen, *Stage Antiquities of the Greeks and Romans*.

80. Balsdon, *Life and Leisure in Ancient Rome*.

81. Allen, *Stage Antiquities of the Greeks and Romans*.

82. Quintilian, *The Training of an Orator*, quoted in Jerome Carcopino, *Daily Life in Ancient Rome: The People and the City at the Height of the Empire*. New Haven, CT: Yale University Press, 1940.

83. Brockett, *History of the Theater*.

84. Tertullian, *On the Public Shows*, quoted in Cheney, *The Theater*.

Chapter 9: To All People in All Ages: The Legacy of Ancient Theater

85. Geisinger, *Plays, Players, and Playwrights*.

86. Geisinger, *Plays, Players, and Playwrights*.

87. Bieber, *The History of the Greek and Roman Theater*.

88. Charles R. Walker, "The Return of Oedipus," in *Sophocles's Oedipus the King and Oedipus at Colonus*. Translated by Charles R. Walker. Garden City, NY: Doubleday, 1966.

89. Bieber, *The History of the Greek and Roman Theater*.

90. Stephen Sondheim, *A Funny Thing Happened on the Way to the Forum*. Produced on Broadway in 1962.

For Further Reading

Roland and Françoise Etienne, *The Search for Ancient Greece*. New York: Harry N. Abrams, 1992. A detailed summary of how scholars through the ages discovered and studied the literature, art, and ideas of the classical Greeks. Contains many colorful illustrations.

Dudley Fitts and Robert Fitzgerald, translators, *The Oedipus Cycle*. New York: Harcourt, Brace and World, 1969. This simple, clear, and straightforward translation provides a good starting point for those interested in reading the classical Greek tragedies. Contains *Oedipus Rex, Oedipus at Colonus*, and *Antigone*. Although Sophocles did not write these as a formal trilogy (as Aeschylus did with the Orestes plays), each one covers a part of the Oedipus legend. Robert Fitzgerald's commentary about Sophocles' style is useful.

Marion Geisinger, *Plays, Players, and Playwrights: An Illustrated History of the Theater*. New York: Hart Publishing, 1971. This well-written, easy-to-read book traces the roots of theater and includes much useful and interesting information about Greek and Roman theaters, actors, playwrights, and production techniques.

Phyllis Hartnoll, *The Concise History of the Theater*. New York: Harry N. Abrams, 1968. A good general theater history with plenty of coverage of the Greeks and Romans.

Homer, *Iliad*. Retold by Barbara Leonie Picard. New York: Oxford University Press, 1960. And *Odyssey*. Retold by Barbara Leonie Picard. New York: Oxford University Press, 1952. Easy-to-follow, quick-moving introductions to Homer's classic works, the themes and characters of which figured so prominently in later Greek plays.

Anthony Marks and Graham Tingay, *The Romans*. London: Usborne Publishing, 1990. An excellent general summary of Roman customs, ideas, people, religion, and institutions, including theater. Contains hundreds of colorful illustrations that bring Roman civilization to life.

Don Nardo, *Ancient Greece; The Roman Republic; The Roman Empire*. San Diego: Lucent Books, 1994. These volumes present comprehensive general overviews of Greek and Roman civilizations, providing background material and a context to understand better the people who produced and attended ancient plays.

Susan Peach and Anne Millard, *The Greeks*. London: Usborne Publishing, 1990. Like *The Romans*, its sister volume by Marks and Tingay, this book contains numerous excellent illustrations that capture the essence of the people and times discussed.

Betty Radice, *Who's Who in the Ancient World: A Handbook to the Survivors of the Greek and Roman Classics*. New York: Penguin Books, 1973. A ready reference that summarizes the important information about the most notable ancients, including those who developed and influenced ancient theater—Thespis, Aeschylus, Pericles, Aristophanes, Menander, Plautus, and Terence, to name only a few.

Additonal Works Consulted

James T. Allen, *Stage Antiquities of the Greeks and Romans and Their Influence.* New York: Cooper Square Publishers, 1963. A scholarly study of Greek and Roman stage conventions and techniques. Contains two chapters tracing the influence of these conventions on later ages.

Aristotle, *Poetics*, in Robert Maynard Hutchins, ed., *The Works of Aristotle*, in *Great Books of the Western World Series.* Chicago: Encyclopaedia Britannica, 1952. Aristotle's essay theorizing on how poetry and theater developed is difficult but worthwhile reading for those interested in learning how one of the most distinguished of the ancients viewed the drama of his own day.

H.C. Baldry, *The Greek Tragic Theater.* New York: W.W. Norton, 1971. A thorough, scholarly study of how Greek tragedy developed.

J.P.V.D. Balsdon, *Life and Leisure in Ancient Rome.* New York: McGraw-Hill, 1969. This detailed look at how the Romans lived and played includes information on Roman theatrical traditions and, in general as background material, provides an understanding of the people who patronized Roman theaters.

Margarete Bieber, *The History of the Greek and Roman Theater.* Princeton, NJ: Princeton University Press, 1961. This classic book is an extremely detailed and scholarly study of ancient theater as told through the evidence collected from paintings on vases and other archaeological sources. Bieber sup- ports her research with numerous photos and drawings.

Oscar G. Brockett, *History of the Theater.* Boston: Allyn & Bacon, 1982. One of the best available general theater histories. Clearly written and well illustrated.

———, *The Theater: An Introduction.* New York: Holt, Rinehart, and Winston, 1969. In this excellent study, Brockett, a noted theater historian, explores the theater as an art form, describing influences through the ages that have made modern drama what it is.

James H. Butler, *The Theater and Drama of Greece and Rome.* San Francisco: Chandler Publishing, 1972. A fine, detailed overview of ancient theater, covering the important playwrights and their works, ancient theaters, and the way the ancients presented plays.

Jerome Carcopino, *Daily Life in Ancient Rome: The People and the City at the Height of the Empire.* New Haven, CT: Yale University Press, 1940. In this classic work, one of the best modern historians of Roman civilization provides a penetrating view of Roman life, customs, and institutions.

Lionel Casson, *Masters of Ancient Comedy.* New York: Macmillan, 1960. Casson, a fine historian and scholar, offers excellent, readable translations of plays by Aristophanes, Menander, Plautus, and Terence, along with lively commentary on the men and their output. Highly recommended.

Sheldon Cheney, *The Theater: Three Thousand Years of Drama, Acting, and Stagecraft.* New York: Tudor Publishing, 1939. Although parts of this aging theater history are somewhat dated, many sections remain among the most thorough and elegantly written descriptions of ancient drama.

F.R. Cowell, *Life in Ancient Rome.* New York: G.P. Putnam's Sons, 1961. A fine summary of ancient Roman people and customs, including a section of entertainments such as theater and chariot races.

Edmund Fuller, *A Pageant of the Theater*, New York: Thomas Y. Crowell, 1965. This rather brief overview of theater history is clearly written, insightful, and sometimes witty.

Jane F. Gardner, *Women in Roman Law and Society.* Indianapolis: Indiana University Press, 1991. A revealing and fascinating study of ancient Roman women, their home lives, duties, pastimes, and social status.

Kevin Guinagh and Alfred Paul Dorjahn, eds., *Latin Literature in Translation.* New York: Longmans, Green, and Company, 1952. An excellent collection of Roman literature, including translations of plays by Plautus, Terence, and Seneca, as well as writings by Julius Caesar, Cicero, Livy, Horace, Martial, Pliny the Younger, Tacitus, Saint Augustine, and others.

Moses Hadas, ed., *The Complete Plays of Aristophanes.* New York: Bantam Books, 1962. Somewhat wordy but worthwhile translations of all eleven of Aristophanes' surviving plays. Includes useful commentary.

Edith Hamilton, *The Greek Way to Western Civilization.* New York: New American Library, 1942. Still one of the finest analyses of Greek ideas and culture, this volume is part of Hamilton's famous trilogy on the classics, which includes *The Roman Way* and *Mythology: Timeless Tales of Gods and Heroes.*

———, *The Roman Way to Western Civilization.* New York: New American Library, 1932. This insightful study by one of the twentieth century's greatest classical scholars contains much useful analysis of Roman playwrights and their works.

Anthony Holden, *Laurence Olivier: A Biography.* New York: Atheneum, 1988. An excellent synopsis of the life and career of the actor, including descriptions of his performances in revivals of ancient plays.

Anna Michailidou, *Knossus: A Complete Guide to the Palace of Minos.* Athens: Ekdotike Athenon, 1993. A modern archaeologist introduces the great palace of Knossus, explaining how it appeared in its original state and how it housed the world's first theater. Nicely illustrated.

Allardyce Nicoll, *World Drama: From Aeschulus to Anouilh.* New York: Harcourt, Brace and Company, 1949. A long, thorough summary of theater history, with many excerpts from plays and useful analyses of these works.

Gilbert Norwood, *Greek Comedy*, New York: Hill and Wang, 1963. This extremely detailed and technical study of ancient Greek playwrights and their works, filled with inscriptions, writings, and play excerpts in the original Greek, is intended for scholars and serious students of the subject.

Whitney J. Oates and Eugene O'Neill Jr., eds., *The Complete Greek Drama*. New York: Random House, 1938. A huge, two-volume work containing translations by various scholars of plays by Aeschylus, Sophocles, Euripides, Aristophanes, and Menander. O'Neill provides a long, well-researched, and interesting commentary.

Arthur Pickard-Cambridge, *The Dramatic Festivals of Athens*. Oxford: Oxford University Press, 1968. Like Norwood's book, this is a technical work supported by excerpts in the original Greek and is intended for scholars.

C.A. Robinson, ed., *An Anthology of Greek Drama*. New York: Holt, Rinehart, and Winston, 1960. Contains translations of Aeschylus's *Agamemnon*, Sophocles' *Oedipus the King* and *Antigone*, Euripides' *Medea* and *Hippolytus*, and Aristophanes' *Lysistrata*.

Paul Roche, translator, *The Orestes Plays of Aeschulus*. New York: New American Library, 1962. Fine translations of *Agamemnon*, *The Libation Bearers*, and *The Eumenides*. Roche's commentary is equally fine.

Sophocles, *Oedipus the King*. Translated by Bernard M.W. Knox. New York: Pocket Books, 1959. An excellent translation; Knox also includes a long and thoughtful commentary on how Greek plays were performed.

Sophocles's Oedipus the King and Oedipus at Colonus. Charles R. Walker, translator. New York: Doubleday, 1966. In addition to his translations of the plays, Walker provides a long and well-researched essay telling how the works were rediscovered and produced in later times.

Rex Warner, translator, *Three Great Plays of Euripides*. New York: New American Library, 1958. One of the most respected modern classical scholars offers readable translations of *Medea*, *Hippolytus*, and *Helen*, and an interesting commentary on Greek play production.

T.B.L. Webster, *Greek Theater Production*. London: Methuen, 1970. A scholarly work summarizing the techniques the ancient Greeks used in presenting plays.

Index

Picture Credits

Cover photo: Archiv für Kunst und Geschichte, Berlin

Alinari/Art Resource, NY, 26, 41 (top), 66, 82

Archiv für Kunst und Geschichte, Berlin, 20, 32, 36, 37, 45

The Bettmann Archive, 16, 31, 43, 63, 68, 76, 80 (top), 85, 88, 90 (both), 94, 96

Foto Marburg/Art Resource, NY, 60 (bottom)

Giraudon/Art Resource, NY, 28

Grafikus, 59

Library of Congress, 11, 18 (both)

Christine Nielsen-Nardo, 25 (both), 27, 35

North Wind Picture Archives, 54, 77

© Ronald Sheridan/Ancient Art & Architecture Collection, 13, 30, 44, 53, 55, 60 (top), 65, 74, 83

Scala/Art Resource, NY, 24, 48, 91

Stock Montage, Inc., 10, 14, 15, 17, 21, 40, 41 (bottom), 47, 50, 62, 69, 73, 79, 86, 87, 92 (both)

UPI/Bettmann, 95

About the Author

Don Nardo is an award-winning writer. His writing credits include short stories, articles, and more than fifty books, including *Lasers, Animation, Eating Disorders, Vitamins and Minerals, The War of 1812, The Extinction of the Dinosaurs, Ancient Greece, The Roman Republic, The Roman Empire*, and biographies of Charles Darwin, Thomas Jefferson, Cleopatra, Jim Thorpe, and John Wayne. Mr. Nardo's interest in the theater began when he appeared as an actor in more than forty stage productions in the 1960s and 1970s. That interest continues with his numerous scripts written for TV and films. He lives with his wife Christine on Cape Cod, Massachusetts.